Genius Born
of Anguish

Contents

To the memory of Dan MacDonald of Toronto—a man who spent his life in service to and among the wounded and the graced.

M.W.H.

To all librarians, but especially the one I know best.

K.B.

Acknowledgements

No book or radio documentary series appears without hard work, a mite of tenacity, more than a dollop of humour, and a cohort of unnamed helpers.

We want to name these helpers; they assisted at the birthing of the book and the radio series, and although it would be extravagant to claim that all was "born of anguish," there is no doubt that without their generous assistance the work wouldn't have appeared.

So first of all, thank you to the Canadian Broadcasting Corporation, especially to Bernie Lucht, Executive Producer of *Ideas,* and Liz Nagy, Associate Producer. Their support and their patience helped us throughout the long gestation of this project. In the CBC archives we were greatly helped by Ken Puley, and in the studio we depended on the skills, ears, and patience of Dave Field, a remarkable and accomplished sound engineer. We were also helped by National Public Radio station KPBS in La Jolla, California, and the Australian Broadcasting Corporation's Gold Coast FM station in Queensland, where Trevor Jackson recorded our interview with Rodleigh Stevens. Our work was greatly enabled by the tireless assistance of Sue Mosteller CSJ, Henri Nouwen's literary executrix. Many of the photographs in this book are housed in the Henri J. M. Nouwen Archives and Research Collection in the John M. Kelly Library at the University of St. Michael's College in the University of Toronto. Under the guidance of the collection's archivist, Gabrielle Earnshaw, we received thoughtful and comprehensive insights and new leads into our subject. We also wish to thank Michael Bramah, head of technical services, Jessica Barr, archives assistant, and Ryan Naylor, reproductions assistant, for their unfailingly thorough support.

For the artwork for chapter 1:

Shoes, Vincent van Gogh, ca 1886, oil on canvas, 38.1 x 45.3 cm, Van Gogh Museum, Amsterdam (Vincent van Gogh Foundation) s46V/1962. F255. This photograph is courtesy of the Van Gogh Museum, Amsterdam.

For the artwork for chapter 2:

The Garden of Saint Paul's Hospital ("The Fall of the Leaves"), Vincent van Gogh, 1889. Oil on canvas, 73.8 x 60.8 cm, Van Gogh Museum, Amsterdam (Vincent van Gogh Foundation) s46V/1962. F651. Photograph also courtesy of the Van Gogh Museum, Amsterdam.

For the artwork for chapter 3:

The Return of the Prodigal Son. Rembrandt Harmensz. van Rijn. Oil on canvas. 262 x 205 cm. Ca 1668. Inv.no. GE-742, The State Hermitage Museum, St. Petersburg. Photograph © The State Hermitage Museum. The photograph is by Vladimir Terebenin, Leonard Kheifets, Yuri Molodkovets and is used with permission.

Photographs:

The Anton T. Boisen portrait is courtesy of the Kansas State Archive and is used with permission.

The photographs on pages 2, 3 (top), 5, 6, 8, 9, 10 (top), 11, 12, 13, 14 (bottom) and 15 (top) of the photo section are courtesy of the Henri J. M. Nouwen Archives and Research Collection, John M. Kelly Library, University of St. Michael's College in the University of Toronto. Used with permission.

The photographs on pages 10 (bottom) and 14 (top) are courtesy of Carolyn Whitney-Brown. Gabrielle Earnshaw provided the two photos on page 1. The photo on page 3 (bottom) is courtesy of Peter Naus. All are used with permission.

All the remaining photographs are courtesy of Kevin Burns; the original page of Henri's Circus Diary on the last page of the photo section is housed in the Henri J. M. Nouwen Archives and Research Collection.

We want to thank Sacred Heart University in Fairfield, Connecticut, for financial support and clerical assistance: in particular, John Petillo, President of Sacred Heart University; Ami Neville, Administrative Assistant to the Vice-President of Mission and Catholic Identity; and all the students—undergraduate and graduate—who participated in the course on Thomas Merton and Henri Nouwen in the Spring term of 2010.

We are especially indebted to all the individuals we interviewed and whose informed commentary and personal reflections speak to the heart of both the radio series and the words contained in the pages of this book.

We want to thank our tireless and astute transcribers, Rebecca and Sarah Higgins, as well as Donna Crilly of Paulist Press and Anne Louise Mahoney of Novalis for their deft and sage editorial oversight.

Finally, we want to especially thank our long-suffering partners, Barbara Clubb and Krystyna Higgins, for their continuing support and limitless patience.

A note about footnotes: All quotations from published material are footnoted throughout this text and appear in the Notes section at the end of the book. We do not footnote any of the excerpts from our recorded interviews, as this material is not publicly available.

Shoes

The caustic and endlessly charming commentator and writer Rex Murphy observed in 2005 that "a culture that offers intellectual hospitality to the chatterings of Dr. Phil and the romps of *Desperate Housewives* doesn't have the stamina to pursue the idea of faith and its agency."[1]

One could substitute any number of reality shows and soap operas and not lose the potency and relevance of his pungent sentiment. Perhaps as meaningfully, spirituality could replace faith and the validity of Murphy's judgment holds steady, although spirituality is a more slippery word, comfort food for the religiously disengaged, and sufficiently broad in application to include almost anything and anyone that could be reasonably argued to improve the human lot—personal and institutional.

The British theater director and Anglican priest James Roose-Evans turns his attention not to the world but to the church when addressing the spiritual deficiencies of our time:

Dom Laurence Freeman, OSB, writing in the *Tablet* said, "It is puzzling and frustrating to try and understand how the mainline Churches, despite all their determination and resources, still seem unable to connect with the profound spiritual needs of our time." Many young people, he says, are ready for idealistic and sacrificial commitment and hungry for inspiration. And yet, instead of discovering in the Church an inclusive vision, and a comprehensive philosophy of life and spirituality, they "dismiss what they find as narrowness of mind, intolerant dogmatism, internal feuding, interdenominational sectarianism, medieval sexism" and, their most damning criticism, "the lack of spiritual depth."[2]

Both Murphy and Roose-Evans are right only in part, for *both* the world and institutional religion have combined to successfully trivialize the genuine pursuit of the heart to know the Other, to transcend the Self in search of integration or holiness, to experience the divine at the core of the human.

The spiritual writer and parish priest Daniel O'Leary understands the dilemma only too well:

Only to the extent that I had explored the inner complexity of my own heart would I ever be of any use to the people I served. I had to learn how to know myself well because it was myself, with my light and shadow, my sins and graces, my pretence and my authenticity, that came across in my preaching, my serving, my leadership.[3]

O'Leary, both as a writer and as a priest, is one of the countless beneficiaries of the life and work of the Dutch priest-psychologist Henri J. M. Nouwen, who was a spiritual writer of dramatic originality and conventional orthodoxy, a Colossus who bestrode the post-conciliar church with few equals.

What follows is a script of a life, a bold experiment in what Nouwen's intellectual mentor, Anton Boisen, would call a "living document." It is biographical, for sure, deploying the skills and methods of the art but ever cognizant of the dangers of the genre. Writer J. D. Salinger once opined to a former lover and would-be

biographer, "Does anyone actually need one more hysterically amusing life assassination by typewriter? Sooner or later you may need to soberly consider whether what you write is serving any purpose but to serve your own ego."[4] Sage, if somewhat ironic, advice coming from a misanthropic recluse and robust egotist. But be assured what you read in these pages does not constitute any mode of assassination by typewriter or desktop, nor that F. Scott Fitzgerald's quip that "biography is the falsest of the arts"[5] enjoys any currency with the authors of this biography.

In speaking of the life and spirituality of Henri Nouwen, one is never far from what his contemporary the historian and spiritual author Donald Nicholl calls:

> ...the agony of being human which consists in the fact that from the very beginning there is implanted in us a longing for unconditional love, for *agape*, which we ourselves are not only powerless to supply but whose nature is infinitely beyond anything human beings can even imagine. So every plan, however radical, to change the human condition—whether by moving mountains or by genetic engineering or by giving away all one's possessions, even one's body—all of that will prove to be nothing unless we receive the Holy Spirit who alone has the power to change human hearts.[6]

The agony of being human, the restless searchings of the heart, these are the compelling motifs of Nouwen's own writing, but laced with autobiographical insight, shifting measures of his tortured peregrination, effusive optimism, boundless energy, and enervating self-doubt: the quintessential post-modern spiritual quester.

To begin at the ending.

It was not what Henri Nouwen expected. His death—which he feared for years—took him by surprise. A generous gift by the Divine Lover. But it wasn't supposed to happen the way it did. It wasn't scheduled in Nouwen's daybook.

On his way to the Hermitage in St. Petersburg, Russia, to shoot a documentary with a Dutch film company, a documentary of his

love affair with the Rembrandt painting *Return of the Prodigal Son*, Nouwen landed in Holland on the first leg of his transatlantic flight, went to his hotel in Hiversum to rest, woke around noon feeling distinctly unwell, and called the front desk. The manager sensed the emergency and called an ambulance, and thus began a Keystone Kops scenario that was only too characteristic of the Nouwen style: because of his very low blood pressure, the fire brigade was summoned and he was defenestrated. Thrown out of the window is an exaggeration: he was actually lowered to the street through the window in a horizontal position, rushed to the hospital, and treated for a heart attack.

Nouwen would recover his strength enough to persuade the hospital staff that he was no longer in danger of imminent death, that his numerous friends from abroad need not scurry en masse to take a flight to the Netherlands as he was resting comfortably, and that there were no obvious grounds for continued anxiety over his health.

But the God with whom Nouwen wrestled throughout his life is a Trickster. Lulled into thinking that any threat to his life had passed, Nouwen succumbed to another heart attack in the early hours of the morning, and despite the heroic efforts of his medical team, he died around 6:00 a.m., Saturday, September 21, 1996.

Then there would be two funerals: one in his native Holland and one in his adopted Canada.

His eulogist at his "first" funeral, conducted at the Cathedral of the Archdiocese of Utrecht, was the philosopher-activist and iconic eminence behind the international L'Arche movement, Jean Vanier.

Graceful, serene, ever unflappable, Vanier spoke with his customary slow eloquence and penetrating insight into the makings of the human heart:

> I want to say something about anguish. We are all frightened by anguish and we all try to protect ourselves from anguish; we all want security. Henri was plunging forward into a world of insecurity. Sometimes I sensed in Henri the wounded heart of Christ. For God is not a secure God up there telling everybody what to

do, but a God in anguish, yearning for love; a God who is not understood, a God on whom people have put labels. Our God is a lover, a wounded lover. This is the mystery of Christ, the wounded lover. And somewhere that is Henri, a wounded lover, yearning to be loved, yearning to announce love.[7]

To give voice to anguish, to sunder the tyranny of fear, to salve the suffering of isolation, to calm the stirrings of despair, this is what for Henri, the "wounded lover, yearning to be loved," became his life's project. This same Henri, a spiritual alpha male, was surprised by death in a Dutch hospital, given the obsequies of an aristocrat of the soul, flown back to the home of his last decade, a home of the broken and ebullient lovers who gave him a taste of the love that eluded him.

A bundle of contradictions? Yes.

Both a romantic and an existentialist? Yes.

Most especially a pioneer of the soul who had what Rex Murphy describes as "the stamina to pursue the idea of faith" and who, as Daniel O'Leary perceptively observes, knew that "only to the extent that [he] explored the inner complexity of [his] own heart would [he] ever be of any use."

Uncommon courage expunged in a lonely and sterile hospital room in September of 1996.

Nouwen's death startled more than himself; friends, family, disciples, and critics found his death staggering in its suddenness. Almost immediately, people began to assess the legacy of a man who was a hodgepodge of both gifts and mysteries.

Ronald Rolheiser, an Oblate priest, theologian, president of the Oblate School of Theology in San Antonio, Texas, and an established and respected spiritual author in his own right, reminds us that Nouwen was a psychologist:

> Henri was a psychologist, but it was not as a psychologist per se whereby he demonstrated his brilliance, creativity, and innovative potential. Still, he was trained as a psychologist, and if you look at

his earliest writing—*Intimacy: Pastoral Psychological Essays* [1969], for instance—you see him deploy a lot of technical terms, but as he develops, you notice that he consciously purges his language of the professional jargon of his discipline. He still draws on his primary psychological insights, but he begins to express them in a more biblical terminology. Although by comparison to some of his peers in psychology—Bianchi, Moore, Kennedy, etc.—Henri was easily dwarfed, they don't dwarf him when it comes to his deep understanding of human nature. I think that what people get from Nouwen is an introduction to their deeper self; he introduces you to yourself, both your noble self as well as your chaotic, pathological, and struggling self. He helps you to realize that you're not sick after all; you're just a human being.

He was a Roman Catholic priest of the Archdiocese of Utrecht, as his brother Laurent reminds us:

Henri was ordained in 1957 at a time when the Roman Catholic Church played a key role in the daily lives of believers. When Henri went to the seminary, he was just one of many of the eldest sons who studied for the priesthood. For example, when he graduated from high school, about ten or a dozen of the thirty boys went to the seminary. It was customary; it was natural; it was the time. And when he was ordained, it was as part of a group of nearly thirty seminarians. The church of the time was highly influential, its place in society prestigious. It simply offered one a promising future.

He was a gay celibate, a point that author, psychotherapist, and former Benedictine monk Richard Sipe takes pains to outline:

Henri, after twenty-five years as a priest, for the first time allows himself to fall in love. In his case, it was with another man, although it was not reciprocated. This intense experience brought many things, unfinished business, if you like, to the fore.

Nouwen was a prolific author, as Gabrielle Earnshaw, the archivist for the Henri J. M. Nouwen Archives and Research Collection,

John M. Kelly Library, University of St. Michael's College in the University of Toronto, notes:

> Of his thirty-nine books, Nouwen wrote three in Dutch and left us, in addition to his primary texts, a database of more than eighteen thousand records representing over one hundred and fifty thousand individual documents and other items, and literally half a Canadian football field of archival boxes. More than seven million copies of his books have been sold worldwide. There are over thirty different language translations of his work. A veritable industry.

Besides being a prolific writer, he was a charismatic speaker and teacher who regularly held his audience or class spellbound. Robert Jonas, a doctoral student at Harvard University when Nouwen was a professor there, subsequently a close friend, and a psychologist and retreat giver of national reputation, observes:

> I was a graduate student in educational psychology at Harvard and I had heard about Henri, how electrifying a speaker and spiritual leader he was. I recall that for some time I put off attending one of his lectures, until finally, along with Margaret, my future wife, her mother, and her mother's Buddhist meditation teacher, we went to hear him at St. Paul's Church in Harvard Square. The basement hall accommodates some five hundred people, and we managed to get four seats in the front row. We were fortunate. The place was full. Henri entered, and in a measured way began to speak about our relationship to God, our belovedness, the centrality of Jesus. He spoke with eloquence, and as he spoke I had a feeling, a gradual, and yet ever-increasing intuition, that the spirit of Jesus was in the hall. Henri was making something real that was invisible and intangible—the realest thing in my heart. I was absolutely in awe of him.

This most real of spiritual writers was also a perennial transient, a restless soul, as his literary executrix, Sister Sue Mosteller of the Congregation of St. Joseph, makes us aware:

> He turned my world inside out. In contrast to me, he had extensive international experiences, a wide and faithful reading public, and

a ready audience for his lectures, retreats, homilies, and keynote addresses. His life was so much bigger than mine, yet he opened me to new vistas.

And, in the end, he was an overwhelmingly singular presence. Jean Vanier:

> He was a spectacularly gifted man. When I say spectacular, I mean as in theatrical, the way he would perform, walking up and down, circumnavigating the hall, gesticulating wildly. He was a spectacle. But more than that. He led people to Jesus because he understood the ineradicable craving for true union that animates all humankind.

No simple man, this Henri Nouwen. The above mosaic of views serves as a prelude to the deeper portrait that follows, a portrait that will identify the salient features of a life trajectory that is eclectic, wild as the wind, fraught with acute crises, a series of turbulent spasms punctuated by moments of liberating grace.

It all began in Nijkerk, Holland, on January 24, 1932—the date of Henri's birth. He was the eldest of four children—Henri, Paul, Laurent, and Laurien—the son of Laurent and Maria, his father a prominent tax law expert and his mother, as was the custom of the time, a housewife, but possessed of an uncommon piety and empathetic intelligence. His family was deeply and sincerely religious, but Henri and his mother especially so. They were also especially close. But as Laurent indicates, in spite of the home being a nurturing environment, a domestic Camelot, the signs of Henri's "neediness" were apparent from the outset:

> I think our mother was the only one he deeply trusted. She was very much the center of his life. Like Henri, our mother was deeply religious. I don't mean only, or even primarily, in the sense of pious devotions and church practice. I mean in the sense that she was inspired, sustained by religious feelings. Henri could understand that and as a consequence they had a bond; he always felt comfortable with her, safe with her, and always able to confide in her. Throughout his whole life Henri constantly questioned himself,

doubted himself, over whether he was really loved, accepted as the person he was. From an early age, he would regularly ask Mother if indeed he *was* loved. In fact, until she died they exchanged letters twice a week, every week.

All his siblings had good relationships with Henri, although our careers were quite different. But I have my personal doubts that our relationships were sufficient. Did we give him what he needed? On the other hand, I have to say Henri did sometimes ask too much.

The early indications that Henri would be needy, endlessly seeking signs of parental love, were there at the beginning. The spiritual writer and pastoral psychologist who would write numerous books and articles exploring the lineaments of love—human and divine—was from the outset clamoring for love's affirming presence. As Laurent is quick to point out:

> My father, I am afraid, gets a bad rap when it comes to Henri. The image of my father as harsh is unfair. He was a highly intelligent man, a hardworking lawyer from a family of modest means and eleven children and not inclined by temperament to displays of emotion. Henri wanted intimacy—from everyone. My father was reserved, and I don't think he was ever jealous of the relationship Henri had with Mother—although it would be understandable if he was. Interestingly, after Mother died, Father started to correspond with Henri, which, although substantial, never achieved the same degree of intimacy as the correspondence with Mother.

Notwithstanding Henri's relentless need for love's palpable demonstration, he grew up in post-Depression, pre-Nazi Holland in a harmonious family environment protected from the social and economic disarray of the 1930s and the ominous political nightmare on the horizon. As biographer Michael O'Laughlin writes:

> Henri was not an unhappy child. He absorbed the security and stimulation of a wonderful childhood home....The atmosphere of the Nouwen home was progressive and orderly. For his part, Henri's father was an articulate intellectual. He was always pondering and

discussing the great topics of the day. Henri's mother was fond of writing and literature. She read widely in several European languages. Together they created an intellectual ambience that provided endless stimulation for the young Henri Nouwen.[8]

Even during the period of the Nazi occupation of the Netherlands, the resistance of the partisans, and the eventual roundup of the Jews by the Gestapo and the SS, the Nouwen children were largely protected from the dangerous reality engulfing them. One incident in particular, involving their father, highlighted how vulnerable everyone was in the Holland of the war years.

Shortly after D-day, German troops forced their way into the Nouwen household looking for the father in order to send him into forced labor. Conscious of the likelihood of something like this happening, Laurent Nouwen, the father, had prepared a hiding place under the windowsill in the attic to avoid capture. When the troops broke into the home looking for him, his native caution, good judgment, and prudent planning ensured his safety. Not as traumatic an encounter with Nazi tyranny as many other Dutch families faced, but nonetheless a reminder of the evil that had overtaken their land.

Much later Nouwen would reflect on the darker implications of Dutch survival in general and his own in particular in "Resisting the Forces of Death":

When the Second World War came to an end, I was only thirteen years old. Although my parents had skillfully protected me and my brother from the horror of the Nazis in my native Holland, they couldn't prevent me from seeing how our Jewish neighbors were led away, and from hearing about concentration camps to which they were deported and from which they never returned. Only in the years after the war did I become aware of the demonic dimensions of the Jewish persecution and learn the word *holocaust*. And now, forty years later, I often ask myself: "Why was there not a massive popular uprising? Why weren't there marches of thousands of people protesting the genocide that was taking place? Why did the millions of religious people not invade the camps and tear down the gas chambers and ovens that were built to annihilate the Jewish people? Why did those who pray, sing hymns, and go to church not resist the powers of evil so visible in their own land?[9]

But these are the musings and probes of a mature writer anguishing over Christian inaction in the face of monstrous cruelty many years after the event. The young Nouwen, however, emerged unscarred by the Occupation and post-war upheaval, going to school, pampered by his grandparents, his life governed by the rituals and rubrics of a tightly knit Catholic community and, of course, like every devout Catholic boy on the planet at the time, "playing priest."

Nouwen's fantasy life as a young child revolved around priesthood and its trappings—the theatre that is the Mass. Robert Jonas:

> He was aware at a very young age that he was destined to be a priest. From the time he was eight he would wear specially sewn robes—a chasuble, alb, amice, maniple, cincture—all miniature versions of the real garments of a priest presiding at Mass. He would cajole his siblings to play the part of the servers and attendees at the Eucharist—you know, the cupbearers, the crucifer, the altar boy who rings the bells at the elevation. They would all gather to set up the table and participate as Henri "performed" his Mass. From the very beginning, as you can see, he identified his vocation as that of a celibate Roman Catholic priest, although he would have little appreciation of what that truly meant.

Not surprisingly, then, the time would come when he would commence his studies for the priestly ministry. Though he was eager to start as soon as he could—technically, he could enter a minor seminary at the age of twelve—his father thought otherwise, and it would be another six years before he entered the minor seminary at Apledoorn for his final year preparatory for entry to the major seminary at Rijsemburg. The regimen included two years of philosophy—logic, rational psychology, epistemology, ontology, cosmology, natural philosophy, metaphysics—to be followed by four years of theology—apologetics, ascetical theology, canon law, dogmatics, liturgy, historical theology, moral theology—by the end of which he would be ordained a priest of the Archdiocese of Utrecht by the Primate of the Netherlands, Bernard Cardinal Alfrink, on July 21, 1957.

The course of studies at both the philosophical and the theological level would have been a standard regimen of studies approved by Rome and set in place for a long time. Strong on Thomistic thinking, categories, and discourse, legalistic in its moral focus, with a strong dependence on defensive argumentation around the irrefutable truths of the Catholic faith, there would have been little in the way of biblical and patristic instruction, and nothing in the area of ecumenism or interfaith studies. Similarly, there would have been no formation in the human sciences, clinical or empirical psychology, anthropology, pastoral studies, or human sexual development. It was a sealed world, insulated from the contaminations of modernity and anything non-Catholic, to say nothing of anything anti-Catholic, regulated in its cycle of prayer, class, intermingling, and supervision, confident in its divine constitution, firm of purpose, triumphalist in its tone, a holy structure disgorging its priests in multiple numbers for service to the Universal Church.

The Catholic Church at the time of Henri's childhood and seminary training had managed to survive the war years intact and was eager to resurrect the *ancien régime* as soon as possible out of the social, economic, and political detritus of the European conflagration. As Henri's colleague and biographer Jurjen Beumer notes in his biography of Nouwen:

> The enormous damage wrought by the Second World War had to be repaired. The 1950s were industrious years, but they were also very traditional. Norms and values, traditions and customs, all reverted to their proper places, both in the church and in society. In contrast to what many had hoped for during the war years, the political and religious establishment tried to return to conditions as they had existed before the war. The confessional pillars (Roman

Catholicism and Protestant Christianity) were rebuilt as if there had been no war. Everyone fell back into the same familiar camp.[10]

Dutch society was neatly bifurcated between the two principal Christian denominations: Catholicism and Protestantism. They ran parallel structures—hospitals, schools, trade unions, professional associations, social services, etc.—all designed to ensure that the coexistence of the two camps would be maintained at the same time as their rigid autonomy was guaranteed.

This was the society Nouwen grew up in: clearly delineated boundaries, tribal independence, and fervently protected spheres. Holland's religio-socio-political world consisted of the harmonious parallel existence of two solitudes. That was his world before the war and that was his world immediately after the war; it would change and it would change profoundly, but that would come later in the 1960s, with the year 1968—the year of European tumult—serving as the key marker of change, if not revolution.

His ordination as a priest would have licensed him to work in this fundamentally sectarian historical and cultural accommodation. But then again it was 1957, and there was no reason to think that this social and religious arrangement could alter or would need to be altered.

Nouwen recounted his ordination moment with affection and romantic fervor in *Can You Drink the Cup?*—the last book published before his death:

> It was Sunday, July 21, 1957. Bernard Alfrink, the Cardinal Arch-bishop and Primate of the Netherlands, laid his hands on my head, dressed me with a white chasuble, and offered me his golden chalice to touch with my hands bound together with a linen cloth. Thus, along with twenty-seven other candidates, I was ordained to the priesthood in St. Catherine's Cathedral in Utrecht. I will never forget the deep emotions that stirred my heart at that moment.[11]

Over three decades later—and shortly before his death—he still remembered the emotion that stirred within him. This isn't simple nostalgia. It is confirmation of the profound attachment he had to his priestly ministry, to his identity as priest, to the romance of the priesthood. In 1957 the rite of presbyteral ordination had been largely untouched for centuries, the notion of the priest as the *alter christus* or other Christ firmly embedded in popular Catholic consciousness, the status of the priest as an elevated and nearly sacrosanct figure in the community unassailable, the unique ontological character or mark of the priesthood beyond dispute.

The highly segregated Catholic world Nouwen would minister to would be inflexible in its rules, definitive in its self-confidence, a microcosmic *societas perfecta*. There were no indications that Nouwen would be anything but a faithful, indeed compliant, priest, but when his archbishop elected to send him for graduate studies to one of the pontifical universities in Rome, Nouwen surprised him by indicating his preference to study psychology at the Catholic University of Nijmegen. Alfrink, a progressive and open-minded prelate, agreed, and so Nouwen began seven years of study at the level of doctoral research. He was in his element. Although psychology was viewed with suspicion by many ecclesiastics—as indeed were all the social sciences—by mid-century, many priests and religious were doing serious graduate work in the profane as opposed to the sacred sciences. Still, their number was small and Nouwen was among the most enthusiastic.

Well into his studies, Nouwen found himself assigned to Monsignor Anton Ramselaar, who was part of Alfrink's entourage to Rome following the opening of the Second Vatican Council in the fall of 1962. Ramselaar was a specialist in Jewish–Catholic relations and Nouwen's uncle. Henri saw his uncle as his priestly exemplar.

Although Pope John XXIII had indicated his intention to convoke an ecumenical council in January of 1959, the actual opening of the Council, the accompanying excitement and anxiety experienced by Catholics throughout the world—but particularly by clerics—was palpable.

The Council would change the face of Catholicism, alter Catholic understanding of what *ecclesia* means, and adopt a pastoral approach to modernity that was distinguished more by its curiosity and charity than by fear and admonition. Jesuit historian John W. O'Malley identifies the two defining characteristics of the Council—*aggiornamento* and *ressourcement*—in *Vatican II: Did Anything Happen?*

> Although they express almost diametrically opposed impulses—the first looking forward, the second backward—they are both geared to change. *Aggiornamento* means updating, or more boldly, modernizing. John XXIII's opening allocution to the council fathers provided a basis for it, which was soon taken up by the progressive wing. Changes needed to be made in the Church to make it more viable in the "new era" that the council assumed was dawning.... *Ressourcement* means return to the sources with a view to making changes that retrieve a more normative past.[12]

Change was in the cards. And the progressive wing pursued change—meaningful, organic, and substantive—with passion and intelligence. The progressives included church leaders like Frings of Cologne, Léger of Montreal, Lercaro of Bologna, Koenig of Vienna, and Suenens of Brussels. Among their number was Alfrink of Utrecht, a biblical scholar of repute and a man who understood in his bones the necessity of informed media coverage, transparency, and accessibility.

> In order that they might keep the public better informed, the editors of the twenty Catholic newspapers in the Netherlands had already approached the Vatican in May, 1961, with a request that it facilitate the work of journalists at the approaching Council. The request stressed the point that if this suggestion were disregarded, the unavoidable result would be false news about the Council.[13]

The editors could count on the cardinal's support. He had every intention of bringing the news of the Council to his people, of keeping the Catholic citizens of the Netherlands up to date with the spirit coursing through the corridors of the Vatican. After all, it was their church, too.

Nouwen could see the politics and spiritual genius of the Council up close; he could see his own bishop as a fearless advocate of collegiality insisting that the curia—the pope's management corps—function in collaboration *with* the bishops and not as clerical mandarins exercising oversight from the Tiber. Alfrink also argued for the creation of a permanent body of bishops engaged in some form of universal ministry of governance—shared with the Vatican—along the lines of the synodal structure of the Eastern Rite churches.

Not surprisingly, the Roman authorities viewed Alfrink with reservation, if not alarm. And given the extraordinary flourishing of activities following the conclusion of the Council in 1965—the creation of the *Dutch Catechism*, the unleashing of repressed energies throughout the Netherlands, official tolerance for an emerging culture of experimentation and prophetic visioning, the breakdown of discipline in some ecclesiastical quarters, the casting off of the bonds of a rigid dogmatism and its replacement with a theological antinomianism—the winds of change generated by the Second Vatican Council seemed like a typhoon so powerful that, once it was spent, the Catholic Church in Holland would be all but unrecognizable.

It was not long after the final session of the Council concluded that a deluge of demands, not only for renewal but also for reform, swept across the Netherlands. Alfrink and his fellow bishops seemed powerless to stem the cries for change. The church was beginning to fracture as much as it was beginning to ferment. The Vatican looked with mounting anxiety on the course of events in hitherto devout Holland.

The creative turmoil that beset post-conciliar Holland and the existential challenges it was compelled to face were articulated with a certain Nietzschean tonality by the Augustinian theologian Robert Adolfs in his 1966 polemic, *The Grave of God: Has the Church a Future?*

The great achievement of the Council and of the so called *aggiornamento* was that attention was drawn to principles by means of which the Church could be structurally adapted in the future, with the result that she would at least no longer give the impression of being an antiquated monument among contemporary secular institutions. This structural adaptation has by no means been accomplished yet, but at least the principles exist, and the possibility of applying these principles.[14]

Confusion and debate about these principles would dominate the Dutch Catholic setting for some time to come; there would be brave and creative outpourings of thought and practice, new catechetical and liturgical publications, a growing polarization within the Catholic population, and efforts by Rome to put the brakes on a church seen to be running amok. The specially convoked Dutch Synod was Rome's response to a situation she perceived as out of control.

Nouwen was nowhere to be found on the continent; he was elsewhere.

Nurtured and inspired by the intellectual intensity of the Council, by its warm and non-judgmental approach to modernity, Nouwen was emboldened to ask Alfrink for permission to do something quite irregular for a Roman Catholic clergyman at the time: apply for a fellowship in religion and psychiatry at the Menninger Foundation in Topeka, Kansas. Alfrink, as he had done earlier when he gave Nouwen permission to pursue graduate studies in psychology at Nijmegen, agreed. Nouwen applied and he was awarded a fellowship.

Peter Naus, a social psychologist and a professor emeritus of St. Jerome's University in the University of Waterloo, Ontario, was an old friend of Nouwen's whose friendship began during the Nijmegen years:

I met Henri in 1957, before the Council just as he was beginning his studies in psychology. I was in my third year and was asked to facilitate discussions among first-year students. That is how I met Henri. He was in year one and I was in year three. We never actually took classes together, but we began to bond around matters that surfaced over my girlfriend and future wife, Anke. She was not a

Roman Catholic and I was at the time a conservative Catholic. We concluded that on a topic as important as religion was—at least for me—we needed to talk about its place in our relationship. We decided that it would be a good idea for her to become more familiar with Roman Catholicism and because, apart from the chaplains, Henri was the priest I knew best, I asked him if he would introduce Anke to Catholicism in a serious and comprehensive way. He agreed; we met on average once a week. This was the true basis of our developing friendship.

Nouwen's involvement with Naus proved to be more than simply a deepening friendship between two university students. It came to involve the growing family:

I don't remember the details of the conversations we three had, but I remember the tone, the colour of it. And what struck me repeatedly, given that I had a very conservative Catholic upbringing, was that this priest, Henri, was really too liberal for me. I recall especially conversations that we had following his instructions for Anke that dealt with ecclesiology, church teachings, and church ritual. I discovered again and again that what I thought was so important wasn't to him. When I think back upon it, he did a marvelous job; the conversations he had with Anke and me constituted an introduction to the life and meaning of the church that was as new and invigorating to Anke as it was to me. In the end, he not only instructed Anke, but received her into the church, witnessed our marriage, and baptized our first son.

There were pressures on the friendship, however, that emerged out of surprising circumstances:

I couldn't type and I remember that I had a paper to prepare for a philosophy and not a psychology course on Freud and neurosis, a philosophical anthropology course, to be precise. Henri wasn't in the course, but he could type quite efficiently. Because the paper had to be typed and not handwritten, Henri offered to type for me. I was thrilled. However, near the end of the typing Henri became quite irritated and complained that this was a lot of work. Too much work. It was one of the very few times that he had displayed impatience in my presence or showed any sign to me that his natural graciousness had limits.

A minor irritant in the larger scheme of things, for sure. Their friendship was grounded on more than their conversations around Catholicism; however, as they progressed in their studies in psychology, they realized that they shared a common approach to their discipline. Neither was inclined to a quantitative, empirical methodology, nor to an abstract philosophical paradigm that neglected the concrete and the personal. They were both keen on phenomenological psychology, an approach dependent on the insights of the philosopher Edmund Husserl, the father of phenomenology. Several of their courses—developmental psychology, psychological pathology, etc.—adopted the phenomenological approach, and they both came not only to be enthralled by the methodology but to incorporate it in their professional work.

> Henri understood the motto of phenomenology—"go back to the thing itself"—as a summons to retrieve, relive, the original experience. His writing betrays his phenomenological bias as he tries to get into the experience of anxiety, the experience of being in a competitive relationship, etc. He thinks and feels as a phenomenologist and not as a behaviorist; as a clinical psychologist he was trained to get into the experience of the patient. To the degree that he was successful in mapping out that experience from the inside, he was able to allow his readers to discover, to recognize, themselves.

Nouwen's predilection for the phenomenological approach, his studies at Nijmegen, his shared interests with Peter Naus, and the permission of Cardinal Alfrink in the penultimate year of the Second Vatican Council to pursue a two-year residency at the Menninger Foundation Clinic meant that he was now poised to encounter one of the formative influences on his life and thought: Anton Boisen.

Christopher De Bono is a Boisen scholar and Catholic theologian who has spent years of research on the relationship that existed between Boisen and Nouwen, the influence of the former on the latter, the seminal insights imparted by the anguished Boisen to the no less anguished disciple. De Bono situates Boisen in Nouwen's universe:

> Boisen was an immensely complex and creative person. He was a bit of a polyglot and a bit of a polymath. He was a forester; he was a Presbyterian minister; he was an astute student of William James and his work in the area of religion and psychology; and he was the founder of the pastoral clinical education movement. Very importantly, he experienced firsthand the anguish of mental illness. He had five psychotic breakdowns and ended his years in a mental health institution, dying in the very place where he had been the chaplain emeritus.

Boisen's own mental health difficulties in great measure drove his research, his insights, and his passion for care. The founder of the pastoral clinical education movement saw himself as the primary locus of investigation: the autobiographical approach allowed him to bring the various strands together to weave a portrait unsparing in its self-honesty. As he wrote in an article entitled "The Form and Content of Schizophrenic Thinking" (1942):

> The point of view from which I approach this problem is that of a student of religion and of sociology who has himself undergone a very severe schizophrenic disturbance and who has since then served fourteen years as chaplain and research worker in two important mental hospitals in the effort to explore the wilderness into which he was thus plunged. What I have to say is therefore an inside view checked by the study of several hundred similar experiences and by a considerable acquaintance with what the doctors have to say regarding the problem.[15]

In his 1960 autobiography, *Out of the Depths*, Boisen was even more direct about his numerous hospitalizations; his effort to draw on his own experience to devise a therapeutic alliance among clergy, health professionals, and patients; and his realization that the struggle for wholeness through one's vulnerabilities and wounds and not despite them is a mode of spiritual wisdom—his mode. And Nouwen's, too.

De Bono recognizes the singular creation that came out of the whirlpool of Boisen's suffering:

> He used to call people, his patients, "living human documents." That is a phrase that has a lot of legs in the pastoral care movement. What he meant was that we need to challenge not just science to take seriously the religious ideas that the clients present us with, but we also need to challenge the church to say that when we as ministers go into mental health centers, we don't "bring" theology to these people. What we actually discover in their lives is something of the revelation of God, something of the search for God. Boisen categorically rejected the autocratic form of top-down ministry and realized that the minister is actually like the scientist determined to discover what is going on.

As a clinician as well as a pastoral educator and an ordained minister, Boisen resolved to insert his own students into the heart of the emotional maelstrom: theirs and that of those to whom they would minister. Nouwen understood Boisen's notion that one's wounds are an aperture to the soul, to healing, to integration. In an article published in 1968, Nouwen wrote of the Boisen method:

> "To be plunged as a patient into a hospital for the insane may be tragedy or it may be an opportunity. For me it has been an opportunity." No better words can express the importance of Boisen's illness, as these opening lines of his main work. Boisen's hospitalization not only was an opportunity for him, but even the focal experience of his life. So far as he was concerned, without it, "there would have been no new light upon the interrelatedness of mental disorder and religious experience. Neither would there have been any clinical training movement." We cannot stress enough the centrality of this experience to Boisen's life and the great ideas and events which came out of it. Everything he did and said that moment was "in light of my own experience."[16]

Nouwen found in Boisen's use of the case method a way of deploying his own phenomenological approach (appropriated during his Nijmegen years), of inserting himself into the experience of others, of attending to the living human documents in a way that brought into a creative symbiosis the psychological needs and the spiritual needs of his clients. Nouwen was so taken by Boisen's work that he intended to write his dissertation on the history and use of the case method in American pastoral education. Key theorists and practitioners like Richard Cabot, Russell Dicks, Wayne Oates, and especially the prolific Seward Hiltner would figure largely in what would be ultimately an incomplete undertaking, but Boisen would be at the heart of its conception.

De Bono recounts the one and only time that Nouwen and Boisen actually met. It was a year before Boisen's death:

> Nouwen meets Boisen in August of 1964 and it is brilliant timing. He arranged for the meeting with the hospital chaplain and is conscious that he will need to be sensitive as Boisen is very frail. It turns out to be a fascinating encounter; Nouwen went with the intention of interviewing Boisen and found himself being interviewed instead. He does succeed, however, in turning the tables. He wants to know who the influences were on his thought, what he means by God, by the "fellowship of the best," of what the highest values are that determine who we are. What is very moving and decisive in the encounter is what impression this had on Nouwen. He remarks that "seeing a man so closely and being able to experience how a deep wound can become a source of beauty, in which even the weaknesses seem to give light, is a reason for thankfulness." Clearly, Nouwen had expected to meet a highly respected and authoritative figure, and what he met was far more moving: a broken man at the end of his life whose personal woundedness gave light and occasion for gratitude.

Nouwen didn't just read *about* Boisen; he *read* Boisen as a living human document.

Boisen entered Nouwen's bloodstream. Nouwen would publish on him; he would pursue doctoral work on his contributions; he would use him as the ideal type for a case study; he would incorporate some of his foundational concepts in his own work. De Bono outlines the many specific ways Nouwen appropriated Boisen:

> In addition to his article on Boisen in *Pastoral Psychology* in 1968, he cites him in his 1971 book—*Creative Ministry: Beyond Professionalism in Teaching, Preaching, Counseling, Organizing, and Celebrating*—and in his 1977 work—*The Living Reminder: Service and Prayer in Memory of Jesus Christ*. Nouwen was trying to understand what it is to be a professional minister, and in these books he reflects on the psychodynamics involved in paying close attention to the living human documents.

> In his 1972 bestseller, *The Wounded Healer: Ministry in Contemporary Society*, Nouwen draws deep from the well of Boisen's pain and insights—although the book is not about Boisen directly—and examines the role of the minister in the context of the personal wound, of the spirituality of hospitality, of the relational dimension of doing good theology.

> In a much later book—*The Inner Voice of Love: A Journey Through Anguish to Freedom* (1996)—when Nouwen narrates the profound pain of personal breakdown, he cannot help but notice that the deeper kind of loneliness that brings us into intimacy with God is different from the loneliness that we may feel when we are isolated, alone without other people. Where have we heard that before? In the Gospels, some of the great spiritual writers of the past—and Nouwen draws on these sources—and we have heard it in Boisen. It is not just ironic that Boisen lived and worked and indeed discovered his vocation in a mental health center, and it is more than coincidence that Nouwen chooses, for what will be the last decade of his life, to depart from the academic towers of excellence where he has made his home to relocate to a community where visible and invisible disabilities are welcomed and celebrated.

Healing, diagnosis, and therapy were situated for Boisen in the personal; the departure point was himself—tormented, struggling, and damaged. Boisen understood—radically, as it happens—that his clients carry within their private history an experience revelatory of God, and the minister needs to *attend*. Boisen's personal wretchedness, his complex pain, provided the primary fodder for his insights and for his hope. For instance, in addition to his numerous hospitalized stays, or perhaps in part because of them, Boisen was seen as a loner as much as a visionary, an eccentric as much as a serious researcher. Unlucky in love—one woman with whom he was in love did not reciprocate, and he remained in a sterile relationship with her for some three decades' duration—and often misunderstood by his colleagues and students—he could be staid, stubborn and stuffy—Boisen was a largely isolated figure for his eighty-nine years.

One can argue that Nouwen's notion of "the wounded healer" originates, at least in some embryonic form, in his reading of and meeting with Boisen, but it is difficult to establish the direct link. Having said that, De Bono speculates based on a linguistic resonance that is as compelling as it is convincing:

> Although there is no direct evidence indicating that Nouwen took the phrase "wounded healer" from Boisen—and I should say that many of Nouwen's biographers have made that connection with only a scant analysis of the evidence, I think there is a connection that emerges out of their encounter in the hospital. Nouwen speaks in *The Wounded Healer* of loneliness as a "deep incision in the surface of our existence which has become an inexhaustible source of beauty and understanding." And then compare with his observation after meeting with Boisen when he speaks of "a deep wound that can become a source of beauty." Linguistic synchronicity? An accidental resonance? Or the moment of gestation?

Nouwen's conceptualization of the "wounded healer" may have a controverted genesis, but what is poignantly valid is the application of the term/category to himself. In one of his final works, Nouwen defined his wound succinctly and in a way that indicated his visceral appreciation of Boisen's subversive charism:

> What to do with this inner wound that is so easily touched and starts bleeding again? It is such a familiar wound. It has been with me for many years. I don't think this wound—this immense need for affection and this immense fear of rejection—will ever go away. It is here to stay, but maybe for a good reason. Perhaps it is a gateway to my salvation, a door to glory, and a passage to freedom.[17]

However he acquired the term, he ran with it; it became one of the crucial concepts in his thinking, as it would be refined, re-applied, and ruthlessly explored with all its ramifications, psychological and spiritual. The realization that we may all have our own specific wounds with their own particular aetiology did not prevent Nouwen from naming loneliness as our common wound, our primal existential condition, and from recognizing that those who minister to others in their woundedness must mediate a deep understanding of their own pain in a way that speaks to their personal authenticity and not to a therapeutic trick or to an ersatz compassion.

Boisen—the man and the oeuvre—was constitutive of Nouwen's vision of suffering and healing, but he was also "unfinished business" on the academic front. In spite of adjustments and allowances, Nouwen never completed his proposed dissertation on pastoral education that would have relied extensively, though not exclusively, on Boisen's work.

Nonetheless, as a letter from Glenn H. Asquith, Jr., of Louisville to Nouwen makes clear, Nouwen had made significant inroads in his study of Boisen and his influence:

> Thank you very much for your gracious loan of your three unpublished manuscripts on Anton Boisen and clinical training…[they] have helped me greatly in terms of putting Boisen's contribution to theological education in clearer perspective. I especially like and agree with your assessment at the end in which you note that Boisen's theological interest was colored by a personal preoccupa-

tion and that it took persons like Seward Hiltner to put Boisen's ideas into effect....I also liked your concluding comment that, of all Boisen's work, his autobiography will be his most lasting contribution because it is in fact the best representation of his method (September 2, 1975).

Nouwen's efforts to finish his doctorate in psychology were unsuccessful, although he did meet all the requirements for the lesser Dutch advanced degree, the *doctorandus*.

Struggles around his unconventional academic life found their correspondence in his identification with the struggles of others—social, political, personal, and communal. Although he arrived in the United States initially for his Menninger Fellowship, he was swept up by the 1960s turmoil that characterized American life, refused to remain insulated in an intellectual laboratory cut off from the strife in the streets, and was quick to demonstrate a justice component that remained a constant throughout his preaching and activist life. A fellow student at the time, Richard Sipe, recalls their time together:

> There were four Catholic priests among the twelve trainees at the Menninger: a Jesuit from Australia, a Dominican, and myself, a Benedictine, from the United States, and Henri from Holland. We came with our different backgrounds and perspectives—a psychologist who had studied under Erik Erikson at Harvard, a moral theologian, a psychotherapist, and a pastoral theologian. But Henri was especially notable in that his social activism translated into taking part in the historic civil rights march from Selma to Montgomery, Alabama. The first one, on March 7, 1965, was blocked at the Edmund Pettus Bridge and there was a brutal repression of the marchers, with many injured. Two weeks later Martin Luther King Jr. called on church leaders and people of faith to gather in Selma for a second march on the capitol. Henri was there. He wrote that "I felt my skin turn black and I slowly began to realize what it means to be black."
>
> In this he was different from the rest of us. Our social activism was easily tempered—mute, even. We were interested, of course,

but Henri plunged right in and taught his American colleagues something about ourselves.

Unconventional though he was in terms of his activist track as a Catholic cleric as well as in terms of his academic career—in the end he designed his own pathway through the thickets of academe—Nouwen did find himself sought after for positions in universities of prominence. For instance, John F. Dos Santos, the director of research programs at the Menninger while Nouwen and Sipe were there, invited Nouwen to join him at the University of Notre Dame, where Dos Santos had been recently hired to establish the university's psychology department and graduate program. And so from 1966 to 1968, Nouwen moved to South Bend, Indiana.

One of the people he was to encounter at Notre Dame, John Garvey, would become a friend of long-standing duration. Garvey, now an Orthodox priest, *Commonweal* columnist, and author, was an undergraduate when he first met Nouwen; he recalls the first exposure and easy convergence of interest with a residual wonder after all these years:

> When Henri came to Notre Dame from the Menninger, he wound up being a very good friend of friends of mine and they spoke of his remarkable gift as a preacher.
>
> It very quickly became the case that when people knew he was going to be presiding at Mass and preaching, they would plan on attending—in great numbers. He was also keenly interested in just being with people, and he would gather with others, probing the latest ideas in contemporary culture—films, literature, plays—and on one particular occasion alluding to Edward Albee's *Who's Afraid of Virginia Woolf?* and noting that the playwright's homosexuality allowed him an outsider status that privileged his observations, giving him a definite perspective on human relationships most of us would miss.

Notre Dame adjusted to Henri and he to it. It was a short but deeply effective reciprocity.

Although he found Notre Dame congenial in so many ways, the need to complete a doctorate weighed heavily on him and he returned to Holland in 1968, where he accepted appointments at the Joint Pastoral Institute, Amsterdam, and the Catholic Theological Institute, Utrecht, at the latter of which he assumed responsibility as Chair of the Department of Behavioral Sciences. In a letter to Garvey, he explained his motivation for pursuing another doctorate, this time one in theology:

> I am planning to take a year off next year and work for a degree in Theology in Holland. I feel a great need to study more and to detach a little from the academic industry. I will probably rent a small apartment in Utrecht and join the less churchy people. I think that many important religious things are happening outside the walls of our church and I would like to experience it (June 1970).

But before he launched on a program of graduate studies in theology that would culminate in the end, as it did earlier with his advanced studies in psychology, in the granting of a *doctorandus* degree, his academic career—in terms of his credentials—fell below expectations. Still, this did not in any way diminish his appeal to American institutions of impressive pedigree. Yale came calling. The Dean of the Divinity School, Colin W. Williams, was persistent in his determination to garner Nouwen for Yale. He wrote Nouwen:

> The wheels at Yale turn slowly, but finally I report the enthusiastic invitation from the faculty for you to join the faculty as Associate Professor of Pastoral Theology....The invitation has behind it the unanimous decision of the faculty-student committee after a thorough search and discussions (May 22, 1970).

Nouwen was receptive but not persuaded. Notre Dame wanted him for one semester every two years; he was reluctant to emigrate permanently, as a full-time appointment would likely make necessary, he wanted to finish his graduate work and "be able to integrate in a responsible way the theological and psychological dimensions of Pastoral Care"; and he was unsure whether to accept an appointment in a field "which is really not my own." But Williams was determined and in a subsequent letter he remarked that Yale would do all that it could "to make it possible for you to come." Nouwen relented.

So began in 1971 a relationship that would prove highly valuable for both parties. He would receive tenure in 1974 and remain at the university for a decade. But before he arrived, Nouwen's first book would appear—*Intimacy: Pastoral Psychological Essays* (1969)—undoubtedly solidifying Dean Williams's appreciation of the quality of his work and validating the decision to offer him an appointment in the Divinity School.

Intimacy introduces in embryonic form five of the key themes that will preoccupy him for the next thirty years:

Loneliness—"We probably have wondered in our many lonesome moments if there is one corner in this competitive demanding world where it is safe to be relaxed, to expose ourselves to someone else, and to give unconditionally."

Homosexuality—"Today the staff [seminary] has become afraid to even warn against particular friendships whereas many students find themselves in energy-devouring personal relationships with roommates or friends and are sometimes made very anxious due to the obvious sexual feelings which have come to their awareness."

Fatigue—"Neurotic fatigue is the result of a way of living which is characterized by hyperawareness, by which man does not rely any longer on his automatic processes, but wants to know what he does from moment to moment."

False kenosis—"Having opened himself to every outsider, there is no room left for the insider...without a spiritual life and a good friend [the priest] is like a sounding brass or a tinkling cymbal."

Ecclesial disconnection—"The churches, in many ways entangled in their own structural problems, often seem hardly ready to respond to the growing need to live a spiritual life. The tragedy is that many find the church more in the way to God than the way to God."[18]

Nouwen managed to condense in the seven chapters that constitute *Intimacy* the predominant issues that he saw surfacing in the community of faith. Some were general and some specific; some inchoate and some carefully articulated; some institutional and some personal; some new in their emergence and some of more ancient lineage. In that it is distinguished by its reliance on the professional discourse of the psychologist, *Intimacy* is unlike subsequent books by Nouwen. John Garvey has made special note of that significant divide and sees in Nouwen's eschewing of technical language his determination to transcend the boundaries of the professionals and speak to the head and the heart of the general reader.

Of note is the dedication: John Eudes. This is John Eudes Bamberger, a Trappist monk, psychiatrist, and close friend who came to understand Nouwen very early in his life, became a spiritual counselor and intimate, and played a significant role in Nouwen's crucial personal struggle to balance the contemplative with the active side of his vocation (as priest and as author).

No easy feat.

In a psychologically penetrative bit of analysis found in a correspondence of November 28, 1965, at which time Bamberger was a monk of the Abbey of Gethsemani, Kentucky, and Nouwen was still at the Menninger Clinic in Kansas, Father John Eudes reveals Nouwen to himself, identifies the dangerous dynamic that governs Nouwen's life, cautions the young Dutch priest to address the tensions that threaten to sunder him spiritually and emotionally, and provides ample evidence that his counsel will be determinative for some time to come:

> I suspect that—beyond the obviously very healthy and wholesome aspects of your warm relations with people and your popularity—there is a measure of self-doubt that leads you to preserve a tension within yourself, and which probably accounts for the extent to which you feel more or less bound to go to social contacts, so as to maintain what you feel is the required effort. Perhaps more

than anything else an understanding of this mechanism would make a more ordered, disciplined life possible for you. We spoke about this already, but I get the impression that you are overlooking it. Naturally, precisely at this time when you are finishing up your work at the Clinic and preparing to leave, this tendency will exert a stronger pull. For that very reason it may be easier for you to examine it more carefully. I have a vague feeling that unless you see this dynamism for what it is you will always find it hard to get more distance between your feelings and your judgment. I think that before any kind of serious ascetic discipline can take the place in your life that it probably ought to have you'll need to get a good look at this *need for reassurance from others that you are loveable.* And find a very direct way of resolving it, rather than the indirect one of popularity and reassurance. A little more insight into this and then probably your genuine powers for the forming of friendships and for social contacts will be a support for your spiritual life, instead of a constant somewhat vague threat.

It is wise to quote from this letter largely because it is an extraordinarily accurate assessment of Nouwen's inner struggles, its contents providing a prescient insight into the sometimes-twisted trajectories that Nouwen will follow in his life, propelled by interior needs and emotional compulsions, the source of which will both elude and torture him. Bamberger understands Nouwen and Nouwen turns to Bamberger as his centering point in the whirligig that is his life. It is 1965.

Nouwen was attracted to the monastic life, undoubtedly because of his romanticism, his need for the "regulated life," and his yearning for the community discipline so markedly missing from his own life and ministry. It is not surprising, then, to find Nouwen drawn to Bamberger's abbey and its most famous resident: Thomas Merton.

Bamberger, in a preface to Nouwen's book *Thomas Merton: Contemplative Critic* (1981), originally published in 1972 as *Pray to Live*, provides the chronology of the relationship:

Henri Nouwen met Merton but once, yet by a sympathy of feeling and perception he has understood the central motivation force of Merton's life: meditation and prayer. He has seen this more truly and profoundly than some who, while claiming to be intimate friends of Merton, have altogether missed the point of his life and work through lack of feeling for his vision of God, humanity, and the cosmos. There is nothing surprising in this fact. True understanding depends not only on intelligence and proximity but above all on the heart.[19]

Nouwen's approach through the heart seems right for him, but he also approached Merton via his diaries, the consummate record of his daily struggles, joys, aspirations, and personal defeats. As Nouwen himself observes in his Merton book:

Merton was the reporter of his own inner life. He put his daily feelings and thoughts under the critical eye of the Gospel and in the depth of solitude he found God and other human beings. This cleansing was necessary before he could detach himself from his preoccupations to touch the world—which was being wrenched apart by racial discrimination, violence, and poverty—with the hand of compassion.[20]

Nouwen, too, was a "reporter of his own inner life"—in some thirty-nine books and a thousand articles, although only a few were as overtly autobiographical as a diary or journal. He came to understand near the end of his life that the woundedness of others, as well as his own woundedness, were not simply existential realities to be recorded, analyzed, probed, and exorcized, *but* a summons to intense and authentic living. He came to appreciate in time that his wounds were not so much "gaping abysses" but "gateways to new life," and that these very gateways constitute a spiritual cartography of their own: they define the terrain, the hills and valleys, contours and lineaments, of a psychological and emotional life aching into holiness.

In this, Merton was his teacher, his inspiration, and his exemplar.

Their unique contributions—the recovery of the contemplative tradition for the larger church, the reclamation of interiority and meditation as crucial ingredients of any meaningful humanist philosophy or anthropology, their commitment to the restitution of vital streams of life largely neglected by the official church, and their theological extraterritoriality—are all a matter of public record, perduring features of their respective legacies, signature notes of their creative, organic, and yes, in many ways foundationally conservative spiritualities.

The American monk and the Dutch priest shared much in common besides their shared legacies:

- they were children of the twentieth century (Thomas Merton: 1915–1968; Henri Nouwen: 1932–1996);

- they were enthralled by the fields of psychology and psychiatry, included numerous experts among their friends and correspondents, and drew on work of the pioneers in each of the disciplines, both to write and to employ for their own benefit (both Merton and Nouwen experienced clinical depression at one point in their respective lives);

- their struggles and crises in relation to sexuality were constitutive of their spiritual journey to maturation and integration;

- they both experienced the dynamic and often contorted tension between solitude and community;

- they both developed a "spirituality of peace-making" that was both all-pervasive and controversial;

- they experienced at its core the exacting demands of compassion in a time of dissolution—personal, social, and ecclesial;

- they feared the soul-destroying power of the cult of celebrity at the same time as it held them in its thrall;

- they remained, throughout their writing lives, quintessentially self-disclosing.

Although there are clear parallels between the two of them, many points of personal convergence, and some shared themes running through their writing, Merton and Nouwen were also starkly unlike, and it is too grandiose and simplistic to see them as easy replications of each other. Bamberger, in particular, in an oral interview he gave biographer Michael Ford, is especially keen on differentiating them, given his own privileged point of access to both:

> Merton was my spiritual director and my teacher, and I worked with him for ten years, so I knew his style very well. Henri's style was very different from Merton's. I think Merton was an unusual type of person; I don't think Henri was.[21]

Bamberger's appreciation of Merton's electric genius, his comprehensive interests, encyclopedic knowledge, and defining gifts as a poet and man of letters is set against the more pedestrian background of the psychologist-priest from Holland. Nouwen's special contribution can be found in the fact that he was in himself a phenomenon—driven by an unchecked passion to solicit love, a charismatic personality, a performance artist in the pulpit and in the lecture hall, a cipher in whom others could see and gauge the measure of their own turmoil. In other words, Merton, the scholar and poet, discloses others to themselves by inviting them into the interiority of word, silence, and stillness. Nouwen, by contrast, captures the theatricality of the Spirit's eruptions by means of the set pieces that make up the drama of his life. His is more the spirituality of the cabaret rather than that of the cloister.

But he learned from the cloister—both Merton and Bamberger spoke to their personal monkhood, by which Raimundo Panikkar, a respected world religions scholar, means a "constitutive dimension of human life." The monk is *the* expression of this archetype, as Panikkar notes, "a unique quality of each person, which at once needs and shuns institutionalization."[22]

Nouwen spent his life desperately needing institutions at the same time as he felt their hold on him to be spiritually stagnating.

And so when he chose to live and work in the Monastery of Our Lady of the Genesee—not as a guest, itinerant travel writer, or spiritual dilettante, but as someone for whom the monastic rule would define the rhythm of his life—such a decision was a pledge of his earnestness in seeking the Hidden God, the *deus absconditus*, and in securing God's intimacy. And helping him once again is his friend John Eudes Bamberger, no longer at Gethsemani, but now abbot of the Genesee monastery.

Still, it is never so simple; the personal urgency that always accompanied Nouwen's quest to corner God would spend itself and remain only marginally successful, but always perfect fodder for the next book.

Out of his sojourn at the monastery would come *The Genesee Diary: Report from a Trappist Monastery*, a work that his friend John Garvey terms his personal favorite:

> I liked the *Diary* for its frankness, its detailed record of the minutiae of daily life—being impatient when the letter he expected didn't arrive, etc. I remember a woman I know who was very upset that Henri revealed himself to be so petty—so human in so many ways—but I explained to her that that's precisely what makes the book so valuable: its honesty in sharing what it is like to live with both awareness of God's presence and the sometimes crushing reality of the dull ordinary truth of our lives.

A chronicle of the mundane juxtaposed with the transcendent, the ordinary with the transporting, *The Genesee Diary* is a modest simulation of Merton's great journal, *The Sign of Jonas*. It is evident how much Nouwen is indebted to the monk-poet of Kentucky: the recording of conversation, rumination, fluctuating emotions, pained efforts to taste God's presence, the highs and lows of concentrated existence. *The Genesee Diary* is Nouwen's literary distillation of his six-month 1974 sabbatical in Piffard, upstate New York; what Gethsemani Abbey was to Merton, Genesee would be to him. The influence of Merton suffuses the book without overwhelming it. Nouwen is determined to find his own voice—it is not simply a pale imitation of the master—and allows himself to be swept up by the natural and liturgical cycles that make up the monk's daily horarium, pushing ambition from his mental and spiritual occupations and resting simply in the decencies of the ordered life.

In an entry dated Monday, December 16, just a few days shy of the end of his monastery sabbatical, Nouwen summarizes what the retreat has meant for him:

> Two things seem central: I am a priest and I am called to study and teach in the field of Christian Spirituality. Since I was six years old I have wanted to be a priest, a desire that never wavered except for the few moments when I was overly impressed by the uniform of a sea captain. Ever since my studies for the priesthood I have felt especially attracted to what was then called "Ascetical and Mystical Theology" and all my other studies in psychology, sociology, and similar fields never seemed fruitful for me unless they led me to a deeper understanding of the questions of the spiritual life.[23]

What this entry highlights is the realization, though still dim to some degree and still marked by the fear of indecision, of Nouwen's growing conviction that the direction his life should take has already been decided. He opted for the study of spirituality, marshaled his scientific studies to that end, and now sees his dream for a priestly service grounded in a marriage of his psychological/clinical interests with his contemplative inclinations as realizable without becoming a monk. Genesee gave him that *clarity*.

In a letter from an emerging spiritual writer of impressive moral integrity, the Australian physician and justice activist Sheila Cassidy, who chronicled her arrest, imprisonment, torture, and rape with excruciating detail in her best-selling autobiographical memoir *Audacity to Believe*, Nouwen could find a soul mate, a companion in anguish. Cassidy wrote to Nouwen on July 30, 1976, extolling the merits of *The Genesee Diary*:

I think the sort of sharing in your book is very brave and very useful. I identify with so much of what you say—longing to be noticed and loved and thought well of. I recently spent some weeks in an enclosed Benedictine convent and experienced so many of the emotions that you relate although wanting as you did to give all.... There seems to be a sort of infused wisdom granted to monastics on mountain tops—all very unfair!...I, too, wondered if I had a vocation to be a contemplative and was both sad and cheated and thankful that I didn't.

Like Nouwen, Cassidy came to understand the Gospel as the Wild Word, shattering the conventions of professional living with unplanned eruptions of the spirit and grace. These eruptions took her variously from the medical faculty at Oxford to the liminal points of human experience and endurance: a torture chamber and a hospice bed, from the Chile of Augusto Pinochet's barbaric rule to the palliative care unit of a hospital in Plymouth, England. The contemplative dimension was never softened or extirpated; it was made subservient to her passionate activism. She could see in Nouwen's anguish something of her own, and that was never better communicated than by means of his blisteringly naked journal entries in *The Genesee Diary*.

Five years after his first stay at the Abbey of the Genesee, Nouwen would return. From February to August 1979, he would relive his earlier Trappist experience at a deeper level. He re-engaged with Father John Eudes Bamberger and realized that *this* time his monastic sojourn would no longer require a diary, weekly meetings with the abbot, or prolonged discernment over whether he had a vocation to the monastic life or not. This time it would be nothing less than the priority of prayer itself.

From the second Genesee sabbatical would come a very different book from the one that emerged from the first stay. *A Cry for Mercy: Prayers from the Genesee* (1981) speaks more eloquently, even when raw in its blanket expression, of the struggles of the author than can be found in the *Diary*. For instance, there is in the unadorned articulation of need expressed in the prayers—and each entry is a prayer—of the tone and timbre of Gerard Manley Hopkins's "terrible sonnets," the Dublin poems that were wrenched from his soul. Nouwen writes:

> Tuesday, February 20: My whole being seemed to be invaded by fear. No peace, no rest; just plain fear: fear of mental breakdown, fear of living the wrong life, fear of rejection and condemnation, and fear of you.

> Sunday, March 18: Am I doomed to die on the wrong side of the abyss? Am I destined to excite others to reach the promised land while remaining unable to enter myself? Sometimes I feel imprisoned by my own insights and "spiritual competence."[24]

These prayers are an adumbration of the "dark night of the soul" that would climax in the late 1980s and give voice to not only the persisting anxieties and priorities that Bamberger addressed in his 1965 letter—the very pitfalls of a spiritual celebrity—but to Nouwen's seeming incapacity to exorcize his interior demons, make peace with his own wounds, and still his restless soul.

If Nouwen was wrestling with intensifying agony over his emotional and spiritual deficiencies during his Yale tenure, his time spent at the Ivy League university was highly productive, cementing his reputation as a spiritual writer and lecturer of growing importance, and providing a theater in which to play out the next act of the Nouwen drama.

Nouwen would remain at Yale for ten years. It proved an easy entrée to an elite world. Margaret Farley, a Yale Professor Emerita and a Sister of Mercy, recalls Nouwen's arrival and smooth progress through the ranks:

> I chaired Henri's tenure committee and it was a shoe-in. Of course there were some cynics who thought his books were not substantial enough, but we followed the academic protocols quite scrupulously—evaluating his publications, evaluating his teaching (there were students on the committee), and getting outside letters

of assessment. As I say, it was a shoe-in. Although he didn't have a doctorate, there was a general desire to truly keep him at Yale on the part of everybody, and the university is very tough on granting tenure and there were no questions raised, even at the level of the Provost.

During his period at Yale, he published some of his most important work on prayer—*Out of Solitude: Three Meditations on the Christian Life* (1974), *Reaching Out: The Three Movements of the Spiritual Life* (1975), *The Living Reminder: Service and Prayer in Memory of Jesus Christ* (1977), *Clowning in Rome: Reflections on Solitude, Celibacy, Prayer and Contemplation* (1979), *The Way of the Heart: Desert Spirituality and Contemporary Ministry* (1981), and *Making all Things New: An Invitation to the Spiritual Life* (1981)—as well as maintaining a grueling schedule of lectures, pastoral consultations via correspondence, guest lectures throughout the country, and an ever-growing demand for his gifts as a homilist.

Margaret Farley remembers him as a genius of spirituality:

Henri was always moving forward, always thinking, his ideas always illuminating. There was nothing boring about him; he was endlessly focused on the "heart" of religion, of faith. The term "spirituality" has become trivialized, in my view, but what Henri was doing was profound: he dealt with the deepest issues facing humankind and sought always to anchor us in hope. Many people do these kinds of things, but Henri did it with depth; there was nothing superficial about the kind of peace he wished to engender. He was not given much to attending to the details—even his driving was terrible—but he could and did concentrate on the larger issues.

However, although his decade at Yale was in so many ways fecund, energy-suffused, and characterized by new visioning and the making of rewarding friendships, there were signs of deep anguish, of mounting uncertainty about the "real" Henri Nouwen, and oppressive loneliness. His brother Laurent recalls from this time:

Henri realized that when he had to give a talk, and there were a thousand people gathered to hear him, that he was of importance to them; he realized the high expectations people had of him when he was lecturing or preaching; he realized that he was in part a performer. He would often go off stage and cry or go back to his hotel room and feel desperately lonely.

Henri did not, in fact, want to be a celebrity. He craved intimacy, not distance or adulation. And he came to loathe the performance part of his ministry, because in the end all it did was to deepen his already all-encompassing loneliness.

The root of this loneliness was not the isolation of the celibate minister or the immigrant academic away from his home. It was more existential than that, more vexatious, more fundamental. Peter Naus underscores what he sees as Nouwen's yet-to-be-acknowledged "thorn in the flesh": his sexual identity.

Henri told Anke and I during a visit in 1978 that he was homosexual. The context in which he told us this was marked by his own profound agony. I began then to appreciate the inner turmoil he must have felt for so many, many years. I can say as well that I personally felt a profound compassion for him. By 1978, I had begun to arrive at different conceptions of sexuality that departed from the conventional paradigms. In the process of more carefully examining the very nature of sexual orientations, I developed a new openness I never had previously. That is not to say that I was free of the inhibitions and preconceptions that I held before, only that I was not blown away by Henri's disclosure and there was a time when I would have been.

But his homosexuality wasn't really the problem; it was his insatiable need for emotional intimacy.

That need would be the primal cause for his restlessness, his discomfiture with his place, with his role, with his body; it would define his spiritual quest for wholeness; it would reconnect him with his own woundedness. Repeatedly "de-housed," as it were, by a need that could never be sated, Nouwen's outward migrations were but one expression of his *peregrinatio* or going forth into strange places. And one of the distinguishing marks of this peregrination was the way he struggled to understand, to accept, his own brokenness as a way of being in the world, an aperture to the irreducible mystery of life itself.

Chapter Two

The Fall of the Leaves

A t the same time that Nouwen found a measure of affirmation in his highly successful teaching career at Yale, despite his eagerness to bring psychology and spirituality into ever-closer dialogue and interaction—"Spirituality without psychology is not anchored; psychology without spirituality is directionless"[1]—and his ever-expanding coterie of acolytes, devotees, and readers, he underwent an especially excruciating period of spiritual trial that lasted for several years.

In a series of letters written by Bamberger throughout 1977, the psychiatrist-monk, spiritual father, and Abbot of Genesee strikes a note of increasing concern over the emotional turmoil that has beset the Yale professor, his seeming incapacity to rise above his "psychological self-hate." Bamberger's compassionate counsel reads like a hybrid of orthodox Freudian analysis laced with the insights of the mystics:

> St. Francis de Sales, in his earlier years, had a trial very similar to yours. Like yours , it was at bottom, a great spiritual trial of faith and of relation to God, but it too had its psychological side and

was reinforced—and even precipitated—by the Jansenist idea of God. You may find it useful to read about his experience (January 20, 1977).

Bamberger concludes his letter by ruefully noting that the founder of Jansenism—the theologian Peter Jansenus—hails from Nouwen's part of the world. Jansenism is a form of Catholic Puritanism, a severe moralism accompanied by a conception of God and God's mercy that is distinguished by its severity. The Jansenist legacy, although an admirable corrective to the laxity that diluted Catholicism's attachment to the heroism of the Gospel, was mostly deleterious in its effects: a flesh-despising asceticism that bordered on a Manichean hatred of the body, an over-reliance on self-abnegation as the primary route to holiness, and a theological conceptualization of God greatly dependent on the Calvinist notion of predestination. The movement was condemned by several pontiffs, but many of its propositions survived for centuries in the religious culture of the Low Countries and in parts of France, Quebec, and Ireland.

Bamberger was persistent in addressing the source of much of Nouwen's spiritual and emotional angst; he recognized that the sexual tensions that surfaced with a savage intensity in the late 1970s were being poorly confronted because of Nouwen's constricting image of God. His sexual anxieties were compounded by his guilt, which in turn was aggravated by his inadequate image of God.

> I am sorry that you continue to be afflicted by your continuing spiritual trial. At bottom it continues to result from your over-stern image of Christ, through your experiencing Him rather by means of your own self-condemning superego than by discovering what His mercy really is (July 8, 1977).

Whatever the origin of his new spiritual trial, it is clear from the correspondence with Bamberger that its enervating effects linger, that Nouwen is adrift, unsure of his direction, and unsettled. He enjoys the university, the opportunities to teach new courses that it provides him, the camaraderie that marks his relationship with faculty and students alike, and the numerous sabbaticals and retreats he takes advantage of remind him of his privileged lot.

Although the Genesee experiences would be formative, they would not quench his thirst for discovering the God who mystifies and perplexes, the very God whose love he is desperate to merit, to assuage the God he fears will judge him as wanting. And so, as is so often the case with Nouwen, he tried new things: doing a stint as a Fellow at the Ecumenical Institute at the Benedictine St. John's University in Collegeville, Minnesota; spending a semester at the Pontifical North American College in Rome (out of which experience would come his 1979 book *Clowning in Rome: Reflections on Solitude, Celibacy, Prayer and Contemplation*); and, following his resignation from the Faculty of Divinity at Yale in 1981, doing something entirely surprising in the sense that it was a radical departure from his comfort zone: he spent six months in Bolivia and Peru. In one sense, of course, such a departure was not surprising at all, but an example of his spiritual consistency. Going to the barrios of South America is not too far a deviation from his activist presence during the Selma March and fully consonant with his personal and priestly commitment to social justice.

Lost now in the struggles of the persecuted and the deprived—struggles for food, freedom, and survival—Nouwen tasted firsthand the pain and suffering he discovered in Peru and Bolivia. Invited by the Maryknoll Fathers to make his base in Lima, Nouwen also spent time in Cochabamba, Bolivia, in a language school and sought to immerse himself at every level in the culture of his new friends. From this time—October 1981 to March 1982—would come yet another book, *¡Gracias! A Latin American Journal,* a chronicle of his ministry to the poor. But, in a manner typical of the Nouwen journey to wholeness, the former Yale professor found himself less the instrument of evangelization and more the beneficiary of the quiet ministry of the others: far less the informed instructor and much more the enthralled student.

Nouwen's guide to his "new world" was none other than the foremost liberation theologian in the Americas, Gustavo Gutiérrez. The great, gentle, and controversial Peruvian theologian enlightened Nouwen so that he could see *with* and *through* the eyes of the oppressed the enveloping compassion and limitless love of the God who eluded him.

Gutiérrez appreciated Nouwen's willingness to plunge into the cut and thrust of daily living for the marginalized, but he also saw in Nouwen both an inexhaustible empathy for the poor and a crippling insufficiency of self-confidence. Depressed, haunted by a feeling of utter uselessness, and reduced, in his own words, to "a stuttering, superfluous presence," Nouwen needed the companionship and generosity of the poor more than they needed his worldly learning and psychological expertise. In a telling observation in his *Latin American Journal* he notes:

> A treasure lies hidden in the soul of Latin America, a spiritual treasure to be recognized as a gift for us who live in the illusion of power and self-control. It is the treasure of gratitude that can help us to break through the walls of our individual and collective self-righteousness and can prevent us from destroying ourselves and our planet in the futile attempt to hold onto what we consider our own. If I have any vocation in Latin America, it is the vocation to receive from the people the gifts they have to offer us and to bring these back up north for our own conversion and healing.[2]

Having understood something of the reciprocity of missionary work, the graced mutuality that defines effective evangelizing, Nouwen prepared to return to the United States realizing that the barrio was no more his permanent residence than the cloister or the halls of academe. He remained restless and unsatisfied at heart.

But his work in Peru and Bolivia—and later Guatemala (where he would go on pilgrimage to Santiago Atitlán, a Mayan town where an American priest, Stanley Rother, had been martyred in 1981)—was not without its own efficaciousness, as Gutiérrez generously allows in an interview he had with biographer Michael Ford:

> He [Nouwen] helped us, as he helped others, to understand the meaning of a spirituality in our concrete situations. And he was such a fine person when it came to understanding suffering. He said that sometimes you had to be close to someone only because that person was suffering. He was exceptional in many ways but especially in helping Christians to be Christians.[3]

Gutiérrez was perceptive in his judgment that Nouwen was not only one of the best spiritual writers of the twentieth century but that he was so precisely because his spirituality was not ethereal, removed, or elitist but rooted in his conviction that social justice and contemplation must be linked to be truly fecund.

In recognizing Nouwen's unique insights into the nature and value of suffering, Gutiérrez underscored the particular quality of empathy—the phenomenological approach as applied to the spiritual life, freeing Nouwen to enter into the lived experience of the other— and in so doing reminded his Dutch friend that his presence among them was an act, no matter how flawed and fractured, of real witness.

Nouwen himself gave an interview in the early 1980s to his friend John Garvey in which he spoke with searing insight into the *mysterium passionis*:

> I think a lot of us, myself included, think that if I suffer, if I am in pain, the only important thing is to be healed of that pain, to be rid of that suffering. I feel that suffering is an interruption of my life. I consider it meaningless, something that prevents me from being who I want to be. So I perceive it as something to get rid of in whatever way I can. I can go to a psychologist, a medical doctor, a counselor, a friend, a lover—it doesn't matter, but in some way or another I want to get rid of the pain. This is quite often our preoccupation, and if we think psychologically we are also concerned with relief from the tension which suffering creates.

But there are deeper questions, deeper concerns. There is the concern not so much to get rid of the pain, but to discover how my suffering, my pain, is connected to God's suffering. In the center of our revelation we have come to know God as a suffering God. Jesus Christ reveals to us that, in him, God is suffering the pains of the world....Then the question is no longer simply, "How can I get rid of my suffering?" The deeper question is, "How can I make the connection between my suffering and God's suffering? How can I learn to recognize in myself, in all of us...that suffering is not simply an interruption of what I should be—healthy, together, good-looking, free of pain—but instead might be a way to my own deeper fulfillment....my pain and my struggles are not just interruptions...but ways to enter into communion with God. Then I realize that compassion in the most profound sense is *suffering with God*; it is an entering into the passion of God.[4]

This is not cheap anthropomorphism, facile devotionalism, or process theology sleight-of-hand; it is Nouwen at his most mystical. His understanding of suffering provides a theology of resistance and integration that can be employed by peace activists working in dangerous situations, ministers counseling the dying and the grieving, and those whose loneliness drives them to seek solace and meaning in their lives by finding in their solitude an identification of their aloneness with the greater human project.

Nouwen's Latin American experiences crystallized his thinking around witness and enriched his appreciation of the universality of the quest for holiness through justice *and* prayer, but these same experiences did not assuage his inner turbulence nor deaden the pain of his emotional insecurity. He was still Henri.

Early upon his return from his sojourn with the Maryknoll missionaries, he went on retreat in Hamden, Connecticut, where he wrote Bamberger a letter of exquisite agony, betraying a level of inner torment that starkly highlighted the discord of heart and spirit that seemed to offer little in the way of cessation:

My prayers and meditations make me more and more aware how hard it is to fully trust Our Lord and to let him really be the center of my life. Everything I read in the Scriptures and in my spiritual reading invites me to let the Lord be my only concern. But everything I experience in my own heart and feel in my own center reveals to me how ambiguous and ambivalent my relationship with God really is. At a very deep level I wonder if I really believe that God loves me and that I can trust fully that love. I keep running into feelings of rejection and depression and keep discovering how much these feelings are connected with my family history, a history that goes far beyond that of my own 50 years of living. Somehow it feels as if my grandparents and great great grandparents and all the way back are part of this deep seated distrust and this deeply rooted feeling of rejection. In this sense I really experience what it means to be caught in the sins of my "fathers" and how great the temptation is to repeat the same evil patterns that have come down to me and wounded me through the generations. I realize that it is possible—by the grace of God—to break this vicious cycle and to let the redeeming love of Christ set me free but I often despair when I turn my eyes towards the complex darkness of the past period (May 21, 1982).

Bamberger would have recognized the source of the anguish. He had already diagnosed it in 1965. Nouwen's language in the letter, however, isn't just another iteration of his lament over his incapacity to taste God's love, but a firm recognition of the pattern that fed his sense of rejection, his emotional projection of this rejection onto God the Father, and his startling disclosure that he can't *trust* God. He is, and not for the first time, more conscious of God's absence than his presence, blinded by the darkness so that the light is utterly obscured. This is classic apophatic mysticism, the *via negativa*, the realization that the movement to love the unknowable and ineffable is a trial that strips the subject of the consolations of concepts, analogies, and intimacy. It is the luminous way of darkness, a special grace, but fraught with dangers: the narcissism that concentrates all suffering in the orbit of the ego, the cultivation of a morbid introspection, and the accompanying paralysis that envelopes the individual in a self-absorbed and extravagant pride, more often than not expressed in self-pitying language. Nouwen had become his own "living document."

Once again in a quandary—should he return to Peru, remain with the Family Brothers in Genesee (a group of laymen and priests who live a life of prayer, community, simplicity, manual labor, and hospitality and who share in the life and rhythm of the monastic horarium, working closely with the abbot and the community as, in the words of St. Benedict, pupils in the "Lord's school of service"), or opt to become a full-time writer—Nouwen was providentially approached by Harvard Divinity School to seriously consider joining the faculty. After much prayer and prolonged discernment, he chose to re-enter the academy. In 1983, he became a Harvard professor.

It is at Harvard that he would form one of the most influential and enduring of his friendships, that with Robert Jonas:

When I met Henri I was a graduate student in educational psychology at Harvard and it was 1983. I had heard that he was a powerful speaker and spiritual leader, yet I put off going to one of his lectures or homilies for quite a time. But then the ideal opportunity arose when he was scheduled to speak at St. Paul's Church in Harvard Square. It was in the basement and the hall holds about five hundred people.

So, determined to get there in time, the woman I was dating at the time and now my wife, Margaret, her mother, Sarah, and her Buddhist meditation teacher, Larry, arrived early and managed to get front row seats.

Nouwen came out and started to speak—slowly—about God and our relationship with God, our belovedness in God made manifest in Jesus. He spoke eloquently, and suddenly I had the feeling, a slow but gradual awareness, that Jesus was in the room, that Henri was making something real that was invisible and that this something was the realest thing in my heart.

And so I became absolutely in awe of this charismatic preacher and teacher. It was a very important moment for me because of my own complex religious journey: I was raised a Lutheran, converted to Catholicism and became a Third Order member of the Carmelites, and then found myself losing my Christian faith and feeling a strong tug to officially become a Buddhist. I was no longer anchored in my Catholicism.

Henri's presence opened my heart and reminded me of the Jesus that I had met when a child. Whenever he mentioned the name Jesus, it was clear to me that he did not mean the historical person but the eternal presence of God—the Jesus who is everywhere, in all time, in everyone's heart. That is the Jesus he re-introduced me to that night in Harvard Square.

Nouwen's electrifying performance transfixed a young man encumbered by his own spiritual angst:

I was taken by his charisma—this long, lanky body with long fingers prancing about the room with incredible spiritual and physical energy. All four of us looked at each other and thought as one: "This guy is a phenomenon."

So after the address I went up to Henri and asked him quite baldly: "Would you be my spiritual director?" I took myself by surprise in doing this, because I am normally a very shy person, but I felt compelled to ask. He said that he didn't know but he thought it might be a good idea to have lunch. And we did precisely that. We had lunch in Harvard Square within the week and I returned to my request that he be my spiritual director. But that conversation—and many subsequent lunches confirmed the direction—resulted in a turning of the tables. I would become his therapist.

Both of us were interested in psychology, I had more familiarity with therapeutic practice than he did, he was in therapy himself, we both recognized that we had similar issues with our parents as we grew up, and so the first chapter in our friendship was defined by this strange twist.

But it didn't really work out. After about a year or two, we realized that Henri was not taking the therapeutic work seriously. I had grave ethical misgivings because of the conditions on which I assumed the responsibility in the first place, given that I had approached him to be my director, so we parted company for about six months—cold turkey—but then we resumed our correspondence, had a few phone calls, and then decided to keep it simple: we would be friends and drop all the professional roles. It had become too complicated.

Their friendship would take many interesting twists and turns that involved their personal lives, their lingering emotional damage, their respective struggles with sexuality and new love. But perhaps nothing quite bonded their friendship more firmly than Rebecca, Jonas's daughter who died within four hours of her birth. It all began with the turmoil of a failed marriage:

Three years after Henri and I met, I wanted to marry Margaret Bullitt and Henri persuaded me to go through the annulment process of the Catholic Church. I was a Roman Catholic and I was divorced, and I was keen on marrying Margaret. I was reluctant to go through the process of obtaining a canonical decree of nullity for my first marriage, but Henri was adamant and urged me to do so.

I filled out the forms, was interviewed by the canon lawyers, and followed the process, but increasingly felt my integrity compromised by a legalistic, rule-bound undertaking conducted by celibates who had no idea about intimacy or marriage as anything other than a legal contract. I lost faith in the process and felt that the whole thing violated my conscience. So I abandoned the process entirely. Henri was upset and once again there was a prolonged silence between us.

But after a while, once he came to love Margaret as he did me, he relented and encouraged us to get married. He came to our wedding but would not officiate as it was an Episcopalian service, and he wanted to comply with the appropriate protocols and respect the wishes of the hierarchy. Henri was like that; he never wanted to upset the Catholic episcopate and respected the rules. Before attending our marriage ceremony, he touched base with the Ordinary of Boston, the now disgraced Bernard Cardinal Law, in order to secure permission.

Incidentally, he never liked Law, who always questioned him on his habit of not wearing a Roman collar, and was disinclined to speak with Henri about Jesus and the spiritual life. But he was the cardinal and Henri did not court controversy with the hierarchy. He got permission to give a post-sermon homily that would be an addendum and not a formal part of the rite. In the end, he was there for us, and he would be again several years later when Margaret gave birth to our second child, Rebecca.

Margaret went into premature labor at the end of July 1992 and was rushed to a hospital in Boston, where she was given an emergency caesarian. Rebecca was delivered, but her lungs were not mature enough to absorb the oxygen she was given, and she died in the arms of her parents in less than four hours. They were devastated. In Robert's despondency, he called out for Henri's help.

I phoned him in England and he spoke with both Margaret and I and said that he would be back in Massachusetts as quickly as he could. He was like that with his friends; whenever there was a crisis, a disaster, a need, he would drop everything and be there for his friends. And so with us.

He spent several days with us, presided over many eucharistic celebrations, and listened quietly to our grief. He always called me Jonas and at one point during his stay he said, "Jonas, you know that Jesus lost Rebecca, too." At first I did not understand what he meant, but then it penetrated deeper and deeper into my consciousness: there was a larger grief that I was participating in, and that it wasn't just *my* loss. He de-centered my grief; he shifted the attention from my ego to a larger space in which God was participating personally in my life, and in everything that I was experiencing, no matter how bad it was.

Henri encouraged Jonas to write about Rebecca, and he did. The result, *Rebecca: A Father's Journey from Grief to Gratitude*, was published in 1996 with a foreword by Nouwen in which he sensitively encapsulated the drama and meaning of Rebecca's death:

> Gradually it dawned on [Jonas] that Rebecca had come to reveal that the mystery of the value of life is not dependent on the hours, days, or years it is lived, nor on the number of people it is connected to, nor on the impact it has on human history. He realized that the value of life is life itself and that the few hours of Rebecca's life were as worthy to be lived as the many hours of the lives of Beethoven, Chagall, and Gandhi, and indeed Jesus....I am so glad the book is here. It proclaims the mystery of life by weaving a tapestry of spiritual wisdom, integrating insights from psychotherapy and prayer, Christianity and Buddhism, medieval mysticism and contemporary spirituality. Rebecca is at the center. She is Jonas's teacher in it all.[5]

By using the phenomenological approach he learned at Nijmegen, deploying the clinical insights that he discovered in his research on Boisen, and drawing on the spiritual wisdom learned from his contemplative moment in Genesee and in the slums and fields of Latin America, Nouwen was able to insert himself into his friend's whirlpool of pain and disorientation without losing his bearings. He knew that Rebecca was at the center of Jonas's spiritual growth and that he was merely a conduit, but he also knew, as did Jonas, that the mark of friendship is co-sympathy, that to be present for another in pain is to be present in that other's pain. This is genuine compassion: to suffer with another is love. It is to be Jesus.

As Jonas suffered, so did Nouwen. But it worked the other way as well. Jonas could see in the agony and interior conflicts of his friend not only the ongoing ambivalence he had over the nature of his ministry, but the persistent restlessness that defined him, a restlessness that compelled him to function as a shape shifter: academic, monk manqué, missionary, extraterritorial writer.

Circus Barum Diary
May 1992

"It's also good that after telling my story to my father and my friends
I now have something I can let them read. Their response will help me discover
the real surprises of their wonderful days and probably ask me enough questions
to make me soon go back. But whether I need to go back or not for learning,
I certainly will go back to visit these fine beautiful artist friends,
who taught me so much of what it means to be a flyer and a catcher."

"The requiem itself was to be held in a large church—the Slovak Catholic Cathedral of the Transfiguration in Markham—and we went there and surrounded the church with vases and vases of sunflowers. The congregation was huge and it was diverse."

"Sometimes I sensed in Henri the wounded heart of Christ."
Jean Vanier at his home at L'Arche, Trosly-Breuil.

"We had no previous experience with constructing coffins, so we built ... a broom closet ... and we made a nice lid, although it was really a door, and attached some handles so that in the end it looked like a respectable coffin."

"We are all frightened by anguish and we all try to protect ourselves from anguish; we all want security. Henri was plunging forward into a world of insecurity."

Jean Vanier giving the eulogy for Henri Nouwen during the Canadian funeral service.

The catcher welcomes the flyer: the Flying Rodleighs in performance.

Henri with Rodleigh Stevens of the Flying Rodleighs. "[I] see in your life many images that can help me understand and explore the meaning of the life of the spirit. Flying, catching, trusting and daring, discipline and cooperation, care for one another and listening to one another, all are part not only of your life, but also of the life of the spirit that I am writing about."

Henri Nouwen the successful author on the international book promotion circuit.

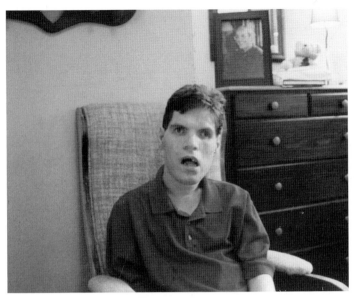

Adam Arnett. Over his shoulder is a portrait of Nouwen.
"Adam was my friend, my teacher, and my guide."

A group shot of the L'Arche Daybreak Community in Richmond Hill, Ontario.
If you look carefully, you will find Henri, second row from the back, at the right.
Henri has a habit of seeming to disappear in group shots.

Bill van Buren, one of the original residents at L'Arche Daybreak, Richmond Hill, Ontario, in conversation with Henri Nouwen shortly after his arrival there.

Robert A. Jonas visits Daybreak with Margaret Bullitt-Jonas, Franz Johna (translator of several Nouwen works), Monica Whitney-Brown, Janet Whitney-Brown, Carolyn Whitney-Brown holding David Whitney-Brown, as a young Sam Bates Jonas looks on.

"So I wonder if maybe being a writer is not more of a vocation than I'm willing to confess."

Henri Nouwen with a group of residents at L'Arche, Trosly-Breuil, France.

Henri Nouwen and Jean Vanier in conversation, L'Arche, Trosly-Breuil, France.
"I felt that for Henri, L'Arche was his potential salvation. but from what I didn't know."

Madame Pauline Vanier and Henri Nouwen
in conversation at L'Arche, Trosly-Breuil, France.
" ... over the months he was here, he bonded with my mother. They would have
long conversations together, and he would frequently say Mass in her room."

For many visitors, this small statue in the courtyard of the main building of L'Arche in Trosly-Breuil, France, is the first thing they see when they arrive.

The first L'Arche "foyer" or home in Trosly-Breuil, France.

"The basement hall accommodates some five hundred people and we managed to get four seats in the front row. We were fortunate. The place was full. Henri entered, and in a measured way began to speak about our relationship to God, our belovedness, the centrality of Jesus."

"... a charismatic and theatrical speaker who lived at L'Arche Daybreak, north of Toronto, and who raced all over the continent giving talks and retreats."

Henri Nouwen, the young university professor.

Henri Nouwen, the charismatic university professor.

Anton T. Boisen

"Boisen was an immensely complex and creative person…
Very importantly, he experienced firsthand the anguish of mental illness."

Christopher De Bono, the researcher looking into the Anton T. Boisen and Henri Nouwen
connection. "Nouwen had expected to meet a highly respected and authoritative figure
and what he met was far more moving: a broken man at the end of his life
whose personal woundedness gives light and occasion for gratitude."

Henri officiates at the wedding of his brother, Paul, and Marina san Giorgi in Nijmegen early in his ministry.

Anke and Peter Naus. "Henri was the priest I knew best. I asked him if he would introduce Anke to Catholicism in a serious and comprehensive way."

Henri Nouwen prepares for the Second Vatican Council.

Henri Nouwen, hammer in hand. A young priest involved in community work.

The Nouwen family home in Nijkirk. A plaque explains that this building,
now a store, is the house where Henri Nouwen was born.

Before taking up his residency at Harvard, Nouwen had queried Bamberger about a vocational call different from the academic, the contemplative, and the justice activist: the writer.

Given that by 1982 he had already written a score of books—many of them bestsellers—it is surprising that he would raise the question of whether he had a vocation as a writer, as one would have thought that self-evident. But not to Nouwen.

> I'd like to share with you the question if writing, after all, is not a true vocation for me. I have taken my writing very seriously and although it seems that I have published a lot, I really have only spent a very small portion of time with that aspect of my life. But as I travel and talk with people I become more and more aware how great the need is for some new insights on the main areas of the Christian life: marriage, friendship, the sacraments (especially the Eucharist), resistance against war, social change, issues around hunger, exploitation and oppression, celibacy, etc., etc., etc. Although an immense amount of material is being published every day it still seems that in all these areas there is an increasing need for spiritual reflection and direction. I often feel that I have something to say in some of these areas even though it might be very tentative and occasional. But I continue to experience a lack of discipline to do it and sometimes an impulsive desire to do more "immediate" things with people here or in other countries. So I wonder if maybe being a writer is not more of a vocation than I'm willing to confess (May 21, 1982).

Although Nouwen is variously coy, self-deprecating, inquiring, and yet self-knowing in his musing aloud to his spiritual father, he is also seeking to solicit from Bamberger some token of affirmation that he is *indeed* a writer, that if the regimented life of a Cistercian monk is not his destiny, his many academic forays legitimate but peripheral, and his evangelizing jaunts to the Americas more than a *divertissement* but less than a life commitment, then maybe, just maybe, writing is his vocation. About his writing he could be ultra-sensitive, as Robert Ellsberg, editor, author, and friend, found out to both his dismay and his enlightenment.

Ellsberg first encountered Nouwen when he visited his sister at Yale in the mid-1970s and was the newly minted editor of *The Catholic Worker*. He went to see Nouwen in his university office at the insistence of his sister, who was gobsmacked by the wonderful Dutch priest everybody was talking about. Ellsberg was swept up by Nouwen, who plied him with manuscripts, copies of his books, and not a little charismatic charm and energized verbiage. Nouwen overload.

Ellsberg, a mere twenty-something, invited the Yale luminary to submit something to the *Catholic Worker*, which Nouwen promptly did: three articles on community. Ellsberg was not impressed; they struck him as "idealistic and a little pious," and given that at that point in his life, on his own admission, "I wasn't particularly interested in spirituality," the stage was set for disappointment and an early lesson on contributor management. Ellsberg undiplomatically inquired of Nouwen whether he had anything else he would like to contribute, implying thereby that the three articles were not to his liking. Nouwen was miffed and Ellsberg had his first lesson in a course on "How to Skillfully Handle Your Authors"—Editing 101.

Although Ellsberg did subsequently publish one of the three submissions, Nouwen never again offered an article to the paper and Ellsberg never invited him to do so. Ellsberg learned his lesson and moved on; but Nouwen didn't, as Ellsberg would discover a few years later.

On the occasion of Nouwen's twenty-fifth anniversary as a priest, at which time he hosted a grand celebration at Genesee, Ellsberg found himself invited to attend, and did so gratefully. Nouwen announced at the celebration that, thanks to Bamberger, the wandering Dutch priest had now found his true home. Not for the first or last time would Nouwen be swept up by his own enthusiasm to eclipse reality. Barely a week later, in a telephone conversation with Ellsberg, Nouwen spoke of his invitation to take a job at Harvard and asked him if he thought it was a good idea. Ellsberg was struck by two things:

the fact that a person of Nouwen's status and position would seek the advice of a neophyte, and hadn't Nouwen, just a short time before, publicly declared Genesee as his home? "Well," Nouwen demurred, "the abbot thought that it wasn't such a good idea for me to do that."

So Nouwen was Harvard-bound, and as it happened, it would prove to be a providential, if somewhat tumultuous, choice, as it would be at Harvard that the maturing relationship between the two friends would now be on the front burner. Ellsberg was in Latin America on a grant, but his girlfriend and future partner, Peggy, was a doctoral student at Harvard Divinity School. Although she was unfamiliar with Nouwen and his work, she was drawn to him because of his struggle for meaningful community. She was feeling a bit bereft because Ellsberg was away. Nouwen was lonely, so she helped him shop for groceries, buy a futon for his apartment, and found herself employed as his private editorial assistant for *¡Gracias!* A stringent editor, she preferred economy to prolixity, which prompted Nouwen to note at one point that the book would be retitled "One Perfect Page, by Henri Nouwen as edited by Peggy." Their friendship deepened; he came more and more to depend on her. Then Robert returned to the States.

> When I was in Latin America I wrote Henri many, many letters telling him what I was doing, and yet I would get these plaintive notes from him complaining that "it has been at least two weeks now and I haven't heard a thing from you. Obviously you are not really thinking of me very much." I was stunned. And then I would get something from him saying that finally three letters have arrived and "I'm so happy." This at the same time as I am experiencing separation from Peggy. And yet, when I did return to Harvard, I was rebuffed. He was annoyed that Peggy was spending less time with him and he began to pout and actually be resentful. He said to Peggy, "You're my friend, and now that Robert has returned suddenly you don't need me anymore." But this passed and when Peggy and I married, Henri was there.

As time passed, Ellsberg would become more involved with Nouwen's writing, especially after he was appointed editor at Orbis Books in 1987. He saw Nouwen's typical pattern replay over and over again—his compulsive activity, his chronic need to fill in time with projects, his anxiety about relationships, his insecurity around the adulation of his fans and readers, his abiding feeling of unworthiness (the feeling that in some way, if they knew who he really was, they would neither love nor respect him), and his scorching self-honesty. Once again he felt the sting of disapproval when Nouwen complained at one point over the paltry sum offered as an advance on a book Orbis was to publish. When Ellsberg responded to Nouwen's lament that he had never been offered so small an advance, that it surely reflected a lack of seriousness on the publisher's part, and that it was a sign of how little they valued his work, he noted that Nouwen had understood in an early conversation that Orbis was not in a position to offer the kind of advances he was accustomed to receiving from his other publishers like Doubleday and Harper, and that Ellsberg was offended by the tone of his complaint. Nouwen, not unsurprisingly, wrote back "Never mind, forget about it and please forgive me." It never happened again.

The incident revealed to Ellsberg Nouwen's emotional volatility, his thin-skinned nature, his sensitivity to any gesture or comment that he perceived as undervaluing his work. It was easy to see why Nouwen's hypersensitive response to criticism was at its highest: he was deeply unhappy at Harvard. Ellsberg confirms Robert Jonas's assessment that the Harvard years were marked by a heightened feeling of dislocation, that this Ivy League university was not Yale.

> Henri's time at the Harvard School of Divinity was not a good time for him. He was a person who wanted to *generate community*, to stimulate and foster a deeper spirituality in his students, to talk about how one cultivates a close relationship with Jesus, and he was doing this at a time when the professoriate and most of the graduate students were keen on biblical hermeneutics, post-structuralism, feminism, and numerous other intellectual trends. As a conse-

quence, Henri was seen by many as a bit of a nut, an evangelizer of some sort, with many speculating why he was at the Harvard School of Divinity at all. He didn't write scholarly books, he taught scripture but spoke neither Greek nor Hebrew, and his standards of grading were below par.

Even though his classes were well attended—he was no less popular than he was as a lecturer at Yale or Notre Dame—he felt that he was largely ignored by his colleagues. He didn't seem to understand that at Harvard he was no more special or famous than any of the others; they, too, were writing books. He never quite appreciated the culture at Harvard: everybody is famous, and no one pays attention to anyone else.

Increasingly, the decision to come to the Divinity School looked to him as a disastrous mistake.

It wasn't that he had failed to inspire students, evoke new loyalties, or embark in new intellectual directions. The feeling of displacement was a compound of many factors, including the iciness of the university, his vocational crisis, and his depressive temperament.

Harvard wasn't really the problem. The problem was Nouwen himself. Ron Rolheiser, an Oblate priest, theologian, and internationally known spiritual writer who self-identifies as a disciple of Nouwen's, provides insight into Nouwen's self-contradictory makeup:

What Henri was able to do is to shine a flashlight and not just a microscopic light onto his own psyche and soul. He laid bare what was there, including its complexity. This is what makes him one of the great spiritual writers: his refusal to ignore our inner complexity. Many spiritual writers elect to write about our humanity in the abstract, sexuality in the abstract. Henri, in contrast, deliberately chose to be radically honest; he could be deeply personal *without* being exhibitionistic; he could self-disclose without engaging in a spiritual striptease.

He acknowledges in his writing that he wants to be a great saint and yet experience every sensation that sinners have, to pray a great deal and still have time for television, to live the revolutionary life of the poor but still have his computer and travel at will. In fact, to quote him, "I need to do all this stuff; I want it all. No wonder my life is such a strained endeavor."

It would indeed be "a strained endeavor" bringing God into a Harvard lecture hall, but that didn't dissuade Nouwen from trying, as Robert Jonas remembers:

Henri would begin his classes with having everybody do a Taizé chant, something pretty much unheard of in most academic classes. He wanted to create community in the sense of the Holy Spirit's presence before commencing class. He felt that such an invocation was the foundation of all good learning; otherwise, people would be in their heads only and nothing could really happen. And he wanted things to happen in his lecture hall; he wanted the Holy Spirit to show up, even at Harvard. You can see why many at the university were uncomfortable with him being there.

If Harvard was increasingly uncomfortable with his presence, Nouwen was equally uncomfortable with himself. Sometimes dubbed the twentieth-century Søren Kierkegaard—full to overflowing with dread, fear, trembling, oracular and exhortative declamations, and profound personal sacrifice—Nouwen's genius was increasingly fed by his anguish. As Rolheiser observed:

He was blessed with a tormented personality, struggling deeply with his self-image, fighting with clinical depression, and not inclined to believe his own press clippings—in fact, his ambivalence over his celebrity status compounded his personal pain: he didn't believe them.

The danger with celebrity, of course, is that you suddenly believe what people are saying about you, and without real self-knowledge, you are held hostage to your celebrity. Henri was always in touch with the fact that press clippings weren't indicators of the person society knows as Henri Nouwen.

In this way, Nouwen's tormented and complex personality was his salvation; his torment was the catalyst that generated and fed his writing and that helped him to delve deeper and deeper into himself.

This finely tuned soul was a bundle of pain and contradiction. For instance, Henri reminds me of the great scholar and catechist Christiane Brusselmans. While a student at Louvain University, I took courses from her, and she was one of the most creative and incredibly generous people I have ever met; her classes were suffused with energy, and when they were over, she would sit down and cry. Likewise, Nouwen—often when a lecture or homily was over, he would retire from the madding crowd and sob.

His ultra-sensitivity, like that of Brusselmans, was a "blessing" one would sometimes prefer to be without.

Like Kierkegaard, Nouwen was an artist, thinking in new ways about religious feeling, ethical commitment, solitary witness, and mysticism. Neither a discursive nor an analytical thinker in the philosophical sense, dismissive of the limitations of a constricted theological discourse or hackneyed psychological jargon, and alight with the Spirit, Nouwen explored ideas by testing their viability, not their conceptual validity. Intuition and not ratiocination was his métier. As Rolheiser makes clear:

> I use the word *artist* when speaking of Henri in two very distinct ways: talent and temperament. The temperament part is clear: unconventional, independent, emotionally volatile if not fragile, single-minded, and unorthodox.

Nouwen was by temperament an artist but, more importantly, and I think that sometimes this is lost when speaking about him, he had the talent of an artist. Think of Anne Frank and Thérèse de Lisieux. Their diaries, *The Diary of Anne Frank* and *The Story of a Soul,* were the diaries of young girls. Now, there are thousands of diaries of young girls that aren't of compelling interest to anybody except their mothers and themselves, so why do these two books stand out? Because they were written by artists. Thérèse had the equivalent of a Grade 7 education, and Anne not much more. It is all in the articulation. Great artists have great talent, and Henri was one of them. I remember the British novelist/philosopher Iris Murdoch saying at one point that "art too has its martyrs, and perhaps the deepest human pain there is on the planet is that of inadequate self-expression." I love that. We all have inadequate self-expression, but Henri had more adequacy than the majority of us.

But Nouwen was also an artist by temperament. As Jung would say, in terms of an archetype, he fit the lover, interested in beauty, creativity, various forms of love, and largely indifferent to politics and commerce. But, as well, artists are often pathologically focused, obsessive, ever poised on the thresholds of experience and wonder; liminal people.

Nouwen wrestled with the contradictions, the tensions, and the polarities that spoke to both his spiritual authenticity and to his artistic makeup. He did this in great measure through his radical simplicity, his ability to cut to the core of our existential agony, our acute loneliness, our desperate search for an enduring and comprehensive love. The common ground of our humanity is not to be found in our political and cultural conflicts and priorities, but in our aching for Love, our inching toward Transcendence. The *sturm und drang* of celebrity, press clippings, religious controversies, and dramatic moral quandaries played out in the public setting with a self-serving panache—these are merely the surface temptations of the spiritual writer. The challenge is to self-disclose without exhibitionism, to probe with integrity yet without voyeurism, to explore the intricacies of the self without narcissism. Nouwen was especially equipped to wend his way through the minefields of delusion and pride because of his recognition of his primal woundedness; unlike Kierkegaard, Nouwen was not a figure of scorn at the hands of the press, not viewed suspiciously by his ecclesiastical superiors, not disposed to wholesale condemnation of institutional hypocrisy, and not physically unprepossessing. But like Kierkegaard, he was passionate about human subjectivity, drawn to the prophetic and mystical dimensions of religious experience, and more concerned about the relational and affective as opposed to the creedal and propositional qualities of religion.

Like the Danish philosopher, Nouwen's tortured cry for personal recognition and validation was simple neither in its genesis nor in its expression. It was complex, like the man himself. Running throughout all his trials and tribulations—and in this, his fate was different in intensity and kind from Kierkegaard's, whose frequent vilification and humiliation by his critics and the public at large was a matter of record—was his rootedness in prayer, his honest if imperfect quest for holiness. Rolheiser situates Nouwen's prayer life within the larger context of his emotional upheaval and spiritual desolation:

> Henri was firmly committed to a life of prayer: he sustained his maniacal schedule without compromising his devotional and sacramental life; he read the classics of the spiritual life; he steeped himself in the mystics. In his own way, he was a spiritual genius and artist like St. John of the Cross, the sixteenth-century poet and contemplative. What is especially informative, for me at least, is Henri's capacity to nurture his simplicity in the midst of his complexity, to attend to his spiritual life at the heart of the maelstrom that was his professional life. A comparison with Mother Teresa of Calcutta is instructive, although I realize comparisons can be dangerous. We know that after her death we discovered her memoirs, which sunder the image we had of her: Mother Teresa just phones it in, she's a saint, that is the way she was born, everything just works for her. But not so.
>
> Her private journals betray a soul at war with its isolation, largely cut off from God's presence, a multi-decade "dark night of the soul." We discovered from her writings that she is immensely complex, that she sustained a living faith in the darkest of chambers. People were shocked and scandalized when they read this of her, a nun shorn of her persona of rock-hard and simple conviction. People asked aloud, "How could this happen to her?" whereas I think the real question should be, "How could this *not* happen to her?"

Likewise with Nouwen. His flesh-and-blood struggles, his anguish, his fear of divine abandonment, his incapacity to taste, to feel that all-encompassing love he spoke of with unwavering conviction, combine to make him a saint-in-the-making, a work-in-progress, a broken and floundering mystic.

Nouwen's personality and history, however, were markedly different from those of Mother Teresa's. Whereas she was the persistent activist and politically savvy church representative—consort of popes, curial cardinals, and Catholic high fliers—Nouwen was by comparison raw and unvarnished, a naïf whose indifference to palace intrigue, ecclesiastical politicking, and institutional skullduggery spoke to his primary and all-consuming pastoral strategy of encountering Christ in the depths of our personal and not organizational brokenness.

Not surprisingly, when he looked for historical figures who embodied for him the essence of the spiritual struggle for wholeness/holiness, it was not from the corps of the canonized that he drew his most pertinent examples, but from that corps of holy misfits, the artists, whose vocational vision exacted a terrible price, for these were his enduring heroes. Perhaps none was more so than the nineteenth-century Dutch painter Vincent van Gogh. Nouwen had taught a highly popular course on van Gogh at Yale—"The Ministry of Vincent van Gogh"—and had amassed a considerable range of materials for the seminar, including the complete list of the letters Vincent sent to his brother Theo, hundreds of slides of his paintings, and a near-comprehensive bibliography of articles and books on the artist and his legacy. They were annotated, highlighted, and meticulously preserved. Nouwen did his homework.

Convinced that his nineteenth-century countryman was a spiritual light in a darkening landscape, Nouwen saw in the wretched pain of his failed loves a Gethsemani agony of great relevance for our time. In one of his few extended published pieces on van Gogh, the foreword to *Van Gogh and God* by Cliff Edwards, Nouwen succinctly outlines his indebtedness to the love-afflicted, failure-haunted minister wannabe:

I experienced connections between Vincent's struggle and my own, and realize more and more that Vincent was becoming my wounded healer. He painted what I had not before dared to look at; he questioned what I had not dared before to speak about; and he entered into the spaces of my heart that I had not dared to come close to. By so doing he brought me in touch with many of my fears and gave me the courage to go further and deeper in my search for a God who loves.[6]

Nouwen discovered the cipher within the life and work of Vincent van Gogh, in the same way that many contemporaries decoded something within Nouwen: a symbol of the turbulent quester, an exemplar of the existential life of faith and emotional risk. By drawing on the pain and genius of van Gogh as poignantly realized in his art and in his letters Nouwen wanted to draw his own students into the *mysterium Dei*:

I still remember how we would spend long hours together in silence, simply gazing at the slides of Vincent's work. I did not try to explain much or analyze much. I simply wanted the students to have a direct experience of the ecstasy and agony of this painter who shared his desperate search for meaning....A similar effect resulted from the reading of Vincent's letters. Their haunting, passionate expression of longing for a God who is tangible and alive, who truly comforts and consoles, and who truly cares for the poor and the suffering brought us in touch with the deepest yearnings of our soul. Vincent's God, so real, so direct, so visible in nature and people, so intensely compassionate, so weak and vulnerable, and so radically loving, was a God we all wanted to come close to.[7]

Nouwen's Vincent renders no account of the theological orthodoxy of his views, the *Weltanschauung*, or the sexual turmoil and twisted pathology that mutilated his life—his Vincent is not ahistorical or immaterial; he is alive and contorted; but he is the Vincent of the paintings, the Vincent of the letters, the Vincent who speaks to him. Once again, we see Nouwen's penchant for inserting himself into the "other," for reducing everything to the relational and affective dimensions and displacing the priority usually accorded ideas, theories, systems, and strategies.

So immersed in the persona of Vincent did Nouwen become that not only did references to the artist surface in correspondence, homilies, and articles, but he also became the subject of a sustained dramatic monologue, with Nouwen performing on stage "his" Vincent, ear-bandaged and accented. Biographer and former student Michael O'Laughlin recounts one of the more unintended comic consequences of Nouwen's one-man show:

> There is a very funny story about his visit to a group of nuns who watched his Vincent performance in confusion and even horror. When he had a chance to ask the organizer what was wrong, she told him, "When we asked you to come give our keynote address about Vincent, we were actually referring to our founder, St. Vincent de Paul!"[8]

Whether dismaying an audience by confounding one Vincent with another or electrifying a class with his passion for a fellow wounded healer, Nouwen's interest in van Gogh reflects that "simplicity in complexity" that Rolheiser sees as a defining characteristic of his personality and spirituality. Nouwen's preference for the visceral over the notional, his attraction to the drama of the soul's epic struggle to find and hold love, and his realization that the cost of discipleship is steep for both the visionary and the mystic help to define and delineate the canvas of his own journey into the heart of mystery.

In a way, Henri and Vincent were soul mates; they formed a brotherhood of the wounded artist. Laurent Nouwen especially remembers how his brother bonded with the disturbed Dutch genius ever on the precipice of ruin and penury, a genius whose racked soul Henri could see as if it was his own.

> Henri was very attracted to van Gogh; they had both been in seminaries studying for ministry, and although Henri would be ordained and Vincent rejected, and their respective religious traditions markedly distinct, they were united in their brokenness. Henri saw him

as a wounded pastor, even if not ordained, a man whose sensitivity Henri could recognize as his own—empathetic, insecure, unwanted, and clamoring for a sign of God's love.

Nouwen had said of van Gogh that "he questioned what I had not before dared to speak about." He could not have anticipated that his self-questioning, his ever-rising feeling of disconnection with who he was, the unresolved dilemma of facing the dread reality of his repressed emotions, his ineffectual sublimations, would surface with greater intensity as the 1980s progressed and life beyond Harvard loomed menacingly on the horizon. His early Harvard friend, Jonas, puts it baldly:

> Henri was gay. I knew that from the beginning of our relationship, and although I'm heterosexual and there was never anything sexual between us, we were very close and there were many times he trusted me more than anybody. I don't know if he said that to others as well, I just know that he said it to me, and that he spoke to me a lot about his sexual struggles, and sometimes I would suggest to him—tentatively, cautiously—that he might want to come out as gay. After all, many of his gay friends wanted him to self-declare, to out himself as it were, and indeed to lead a movement within the Roman Catholic Church that would help to create a more gay-friendly communion. They felt he had an obligation almost to do this, because of his prominence and influence, and told him that by keeping his sexual orientation hidden, he was frustrating, hindering, such a vital movement in the church.
>
> I advised him to come out and told him many of us would support him. But he was so fully committed to his Catholic priestly identity, faithful to his celibate state, that that wasn't going to happen. The pressure peaked in the '80s, subsided briefly in the early '90s, and then returned close to his death. By 1996, he was in great anguish about the question.

Distress over his sexuality was compounded by the feelings of disjunction he faced daily as a Harvard professor unhappy to be at

Harvard. The university wanted him to be something he would not, could not, be, and appeared impatient with his public success at the expense of their customary rigor. He was the subjectivist in an objectivist universe. Like his friend the Quaker sociologist Parker J. Palmer, Nouwen was distressed by the "violence of our knowledge" and the preferred academic paradigm that removed students and teachers from a relational and interactive mode of knowing and being.

> Truth *is* personal, truth *is* communal, truth *is* mutual or reciprocal, and so truth is inevitably transformational. I *will* be changed by truth, and there is no way to evade that. It will be a daily struggle with what I know, to live my life more fully and more deeply.... objectivism allows us always to be the changers and never the changed. It gives us the illusion that we can reach into any domain we wish and manipulate it without ever allowing that domain to speak back to us in a compelling way.[9]

Like Palmer, Nouwen deplored the tyranny of a detached knowledge, the use of knowing to exploit, the reduction of learning to utility. Students and faculty are both enslaved by an epistemology shorn of the subjective, the personal, the relational; they are held captive to the illusion that knowledge is power and not liberation.

Nouwen's years at Harvard were not without their fecundity. There were many students who came under his influence, whom he befriended, and whose hopes he nurtured. Nevertheless, the overriding impression he retained from his tenure was his failure to break into the competitive, success-oriented enclave of faculty and students for whom spirituality was only so much twaddle. Harvard came to represent for him the pinnacle of university arrogance, its undiluted focus on achievement the death knell of the soul:

> One of the saddest aspects of the lives of many students is that they always feel pressured. The irony is that those who have the luxury of spending time reading the great books of our culture and exploring the intricate beauty of creation find themselves always fighting deadlines. Students complain about the number of pages

they have to read or write, and anxiously wonder how they will finish their assignments on time. The word "school," which comes from "schola" (meaning: free time), reminds us that schools were originally meant to interrupt a busy existence and create some space to contemplate the mysteries of life. Today they have become the arena for a hectic race to accomplish as much as possible, and to acquire in a short period the necessary tools to survive the great battle of human life. Books written to be savored slowly are read hastily to fulfill a requirement, paintings made to be seen with a contemplative eye are taken in as part of a necessary art appreciation course, and music composed to be enjoyed at leisure is listened to in order to identify a period or style. Thus, colleges and universities meant to be places for quiet learning have become places of fierce competition, in which the rewards go to those who produce the most and the best.[10]

Having spent a couple of decades as a university professor, Nouwen had yet to acclimate fully to academic culture in general. In fact, by the time of his Harvard stint, he was dissatisfied with what it could offer. He was persuaded that its ethos ran counter to its original purpose, and was sadly convinced that having drifted so radically from its roots, far from the vision of such thinkers as John Henry Newman, Jean Leclercq, Josef Pieper, and Ivan Illich, the university and the culture it supported had become alien to the humanizing impulse at its genesis. There was no place for the heart in the contemporary university and therefore no place for Henri Nouwen.

Nouwen once again pondered his options, rather earlier than he planned (he had spent a decade at Yale and barely three years at Harvard). His restlessness profoundly augmented by his expanding disquiet, roiled by his sexual angst, adrift in an academy that had little tolerance for his romantic values, and increasingly lonely, he wrote that he felt no regrets about his time at Harvard, a sentiment strikingly at odds with his professed reasons for leaving:

> My decision to leave Harvard was a difficult one. For many months I was not sure if I would be following or betraying my vocation by

leaving. The outer voices kept saying, "You can do so much good here. People need you!" The inner voices kept saying, "What good is it to preach the Gospel to others while losing your own soul?" Finally, I realized that my increasing inner darkness, my feelings of being rejected by some of my students, colleagues, friends, and even God, my inordinate need for affirmation and affection, and my deep sense of not belonging were clear signs that I was not following the way of God's spirit. The fruits of the spirit are not sadness, loneliness, and separation, but joy, solitude, and community. After I decided to leave Harvard, I was surprised that it had taken me so long to come to that decision. As soon as I left, I felt so much inner freedom, so much joy and new energy, that I could look back on my former life as a prison in which I had locked myself.[11]

Resolved at last to leave an institution that caused him much pain—although it was the locus rather than the cause of such pain—Nouwen remained strangely ambivalent when writing about his feelings concerning the university. It is almost as if, that once he allowed his real emotions to surface, they must instantly be held in check by professions of gratitude, affection, and regret. The problem, however, is that this need to compensate for his disappointment rings false to his true self.

Harvard was an experiment that failed, and it was time to find a new home. But he was also adrift in more ways than one, his wounds festering, his God increasingly remote. As Laurent observed:

This was a time when his "thorn in the flesh" had become even more painful. His realization that he was gay and that there were people who expected him to be open about it—indeed, pressure to be open increased to the breaking point—led him to question the source of his vulnerability, to address the personal in new and lacerating ways.

And the one way that would present itself to pluck him *deus ex machina*-like from the tempest of his current reality was the opportunity of going to spend some time with the philosopher, humanitarian and charismatic lay leader Jean Vanier in his home in Trosly-Breuil, France, the foundational seat of the international L'Arche movement, a community of and for people with disabilities, most specifically the intellectually challenged. Nouwen was aware of Vanier's work, had met him on a retreat in Illinois, knew some of his colleagues and friends, and was familiar with a seminal article by Vanier published in 1981 in *Lumen Vitae: International Review of Religious Education* entitled "A Wound Deep in Man's Heart." A copy of this article he carefully highlighted and underscored, singling out for attention key passages that spoke to him with special poignancy and pertinence:

- "For anyone who's never enjoyed a stable relationship, there's a kind of unquenchable longing to make it, but at the same time a fear, a real fear of relating. Yes, there's both an enormous longing and a terrible fear. You find this tension in many disturbed children, this anguish of 'not daring to believe that it's true.'"

- "What has impressed me most…during these years at L'Arche is the wound in the heart of those who've never been loved because somewhere in their being there's an illness; for social or other reasons they've been deprived of love; they've been rejected and they've lost their self-confidence."

- "What has impressed me most…is the extraordinary vulnerability, the fragility, in the heart of those who *do* succeed, the powerful, the rich; they don't know what to do because they feel insecure at heart and they have too little confidence in their own capacity for loving."

- "A great deal of activity in our world, a great deal of hyperactivity, comes from the avoidance of relationships: we're afraid of encountering people, of striking up friendships with them, of feeling responsible for them, of sharing our weaknesses and becoming dependent on one another."

- "The person, on the other hand, doesn't give me [a] sense of security, because I don't know how he's going to react to me."

- "How quickly people flee from the human reality, how quickly they flee from their own fragility, how readily they refuse to accept themselves as they are, whether young or old."

- "Fantasy is an attempt to run away from something. Hope stems from the acceptance of reality as it is."

- "Don't be afraid of your weaknesses, don't be afraid! For it's at the heart of your frailty that you'll discover the presence of God."

- "We have to rediscover in the depths of our heart those childlike qualities that spring from this wound, from this frailty, because we know that God is a Father and that we're safe."

- "The basic difference between Marxist-Hegelian thinking and the message of Jesus Christ is that, for Jesus, everything begins with trust; for the Marxist, everything begins with aggression and conflict."[12]

The above passages were all underlined or otherwise identified as key insights that struck a chord with Nouwen. They speak to the anti-Nietzschean thrust of Vanier's thinking, to his reversal of the "transvaluation of all values," to his repudiation of the false certainties that tempt our desperate hearts, to his realization that it is *through* and not in spite of our inner wound that we taste the goodness and all-encompassing love of God, and to his awareness that the abiding fear we have of relating to others, the ontological loneliness that keeps us fundamentally insecure irrespective of the structures and fantasies we put in place to insulate us from our primal wound, is corrosive and unforgiving.

Realizing that there was so much in Vanier's thinking that was liberating and restorative, Nouwen readily accepted the invitation to come to France for an extended time, to come to the very place where it all began in 1964. Vanier himself observed:

I think that at Harvard he had hit a brick wall. I didn't know at the time what that brick wall was, and frankly I didn't ask. But I realized it had to be about more than Harvard. I felt that for Henri,

L'Arche was his potential salvation, but from what I didn't know. I wondered: was it the teaching situation, or was it that he lacked the right relationships? Whatever it was, I thought he would benefit from coming to spend time with us in France—there would be no expectations on our part, nor need there be any on his—he'd have a nice room, and plenty of time to write. He would also have occasion to meet with me.

Just as important, he would have time with Jean's mother, Pauline, a formidable person in her own right, wife of the former Governor General of Canada, Georges Vanier, and a person of astonishing dignity, political astuteness, and spiritual wisdom.

He lived with my mother and I think that at first it proved as painful for him as it was for her. Just getting adjusted to a new shared living relationship was a trial. For instance, Henri thought nothing of taking my mother's cheese out of the fridge, not a big thing, admittedly, but it was my mother's cheese. You know the reality.

At the same time, over the months he was here, he bonded with my mother. They would have long conversations together, he would frequently say Mass in her room, and at one point, she successfully motivated him to write, although the accurate word should be *goaded*, a book on her favorite devotion: the Sacred Heart of Jesus. Although he took the book in a slightly different direction than originally envisioned [it was published in 1989 as *Heart Speaks to Heart: Three Gospel Meditations on Jesus*], he remained faithful to my mother's injunction to let the heart of Jesus touch his own heart.

The time he spent at Trosly—August 1985 to July 1986—proved to be a threshold moment for Nouwen. His university career behind him, life as a consecrated contemplative not in the cards, and a return to the Archdiocese of Utrecht without any appeal or urgency, Nouwen was once again looking to settle somewhere. But it wasn't just a *space* he needed; he needed a *purpose*. Vanier saw in him not only a lonely man, but a lost man:

What I found very quickly once he came to Trosly was how very lonely he was. He yearned to meet people, lusted for conversation—for example he would spend hours loitering in the corridors; he was a man in search of meaning.

We would go out for walks in the forest, and sometimes we would even get lost, and rarely did I find our talk yielded great insight, spiritual gems. He was a man who had come to find rest, he was bent on re-finding himself, and like on our walks in the forest, he was intent on finding his way back.

Helping Nouwen find his way back meant issuing an invitation to come, live, and minister at Daybreak, the L'Arche community located in Richmond Hill in Ontario, an invitation Nouwen was thrilled to accept. After all, it meant that he could move from the House of Fear to the House of Love; living among those he called "the true barometers of the spirit," he could find the joy, the intimacy, and the ecstasy that had eluded him for so many years. He had a foretaste of what would await him at Daybreak because of his time at Trosly, and he knew it would be difficult. But it would also be his new "true home":

> Living with Jean Vanier and his handicapped people, I realize how success-oriented I am. Living with men and women who cannot compete in the worlds of business, industry, sports, or academics, but for whom dressing, walking, speaking, eating, drinking, and playing are the main "accomplishments," is extremely frustrating for me. I may have come to the theoretical insight that being is more important than doing, but when asked to just be with people who can do very little I realize how far I am from the realization of that insight. Thus, the handicapped have become my teachers, telling me in many different ways that productivity is something other than fecundity. Some of us might be productive and others not, but we are called to bear fruit; fruitfulness is a true quality of love.[13]

Nouwen was about to become fruitful in new ways, to join the company of the wounded, to learn afresh the meaning of vulnerability.

He was about to begin the last decade of his life; and it wasn't going to be easy.

Chapter Three

The Return of the Prodigal Son

A nd so, with the kind of enthusiasm characteristic of Nouwen as he launched into a new venture, although slightly tempered by his insecurity around an undertaking utterly unlike those in which he had been previously engaged, the wandering priest of Utrecht would spend the last years of his life with the "holy hearts that know how to adore."[1]

Convinced that his time in Trosly was a fruitful prelude to a greater involvement in the ministry and vision of Jean Vanier, Nouwen accepted the position of pastor at L'Arche Daybreak in Richmond Hill, a sanctuary, a home, a meeting place, and a catalyst for many of the unresolved emotions and ideas bubbling beneath the thin surface of his ego and consciousness. As Nathan Ball, past Executive Director of the L'Arche Canada Foundation, and for many years a leader at the Daybreak community, succinctly puts it:

> A L'Arche community like Daybreak consists of a group of people who have decided to open one, two, three, five, or more homes in which people with an intellectual disability and young caregivers or helpers known as assistants live together in a family-style way.

These homes are typically in normal residential neighborhoods and there are dozens and dozens of them in Canada alone and hundreds internationally.

When you walk into a L'Arche home, you would knock on the door first as you would normally and someone would open the door, welcome you in hospitably and, if you were to stay there for a few hours, you would witness warm, normal, everyday relationships between people with disabilities and the young assistants. Cooking, cleaning, sharing their meals together, talking, laughing, even the occasional disagreement, all this is the L'Arche reality, its philosophy, its core, its pedagogy: every human being has the need to belong and this is a universal value.

So our response as a L'Arche community to the plight of people with disabilities is not first of all to provide them with a service, an employment program, or a stipend, but to say loud and clear that "we want, *with* you, to create a place of belonging." And in the end it turns out that what is good for the persons with disabilities is good for all the people living with and caring for them.

At Daybreak, he would work with the new and devoted friends who would accompany him for the last ten years of his life: Sue Mosteller, Nathan Ball, Carolyn and Geoffrey Whitney-Brown, Adam Arnett, Joe Vorstermans, and many others as well. Daybreak would be his Jerusalem; it is where he would find peace and a new level of suffering.

The Canadian-Jamaican Jesuit Bill Clarke sees Daybreak as the locus of Nouwen's greater and expansive compassion:

I had met Henri before he arrived at Daybreak, when he was in Chicago in the early 80s and then later at a L'Arche retreat in Honduras. I was struck repeatedly by three things: his frenetic pace, his deep insecurities, and his profound, and I mean profound, compassion. Let me give a specific example.

A South African man I know had suffered a great deal from living under apartheid—he was forced to live under false pretenses, classified as a white even though he was not. Living this lie could exact terrible consequences as he married a white, and if he was discovered he would face serious criminal charges. In addition to the pain caused by this fundamental lie, he was treated badly by his father, an unloving and vicious man. He was in a bad way. And even though he was now in exile living in Toronto, he carried the wounds of deception and rejection within him.

And then one day, while watching television, he saw Henri and was so touched by his openness and energy, he contacted him and arranged to see him at Daybreak. Henri welcomed him with great warmth, took him to lunch, and listened patiently and with beautiful sympathy to the man's whole story, and in a way that he had never been listened to before.

Henri also took him to meet one of the core members of the community, Gord Henry, a young man he knew would help his visitor gain distance and perspective. And it worked. The South African émigré was able, like Lazarus, to come to new life, to live the truth of who he was, to break the bonds that paralyzed him. That is what Henri's gift of compassion could do for others: liberate them from the lies that shackle them.

This Daybreak, then, would be his pastoral clinic, his way station of the spirit, and his intimation of God's reign. In an acceptance speech for an honorary doctorate from Chicago's Catholic Theological Union in 1994, Nouwen encapsulated his reasoning for choosing to live his life in a L'Arche home:

> After twenty years in teaching, I felt a strong desire to live in community and to be close to those who are marginal in society. People with handicaps teach me that being is more important than doing, the heart is more important than the mind, and caring together is better than caring alone.[2]

Perhaps no one has captured the "essence" of the L'Arche genius more effectively than the lawyer-poet James Clarke (no relation to Bill). A judge, father, essayist, and poet, Clarke chronicled his

experience with L'Arche in a human record charged with love—
L'Arche Journal: A Family's Experience in Jean Vanier's Community
(1973)—using the metaphor of a stained glass window to illustrate his
point. He observed that Beauvais Cathedral's interior—dark, lifeless,
and forbidding—as seen through the stained glass windows from the
outside, is seen from within and through these very same windows
as a space of dazzling light. It is all in the perspective.

Living in a L'Arche community is seeing

…a world beyond the rule, the screen, the mask—it is seeing a
world where people open themselves up in a spontaneous way, no
contrivance, no artifice, no strategizing, everything is communica-
tion, the priority is always love.

The people in this world are uninterested in impressing you with
achievements and credentials. They are just themselves—broken
and without cosmetics or rationalization. Importantly, they enabled
me to accept my own brokenness as a human being and empowered
me to relate to them precisely as broken, a fellow human being
with his own infirmities, unjudged, unconditionally accepted. They
helped me see beyond the easy divisions we put in place between
the well and the unwell, and they gave me the courage to relate to
them not in spite of my frailties, but in and through them.

This then was the brave new world Nouwen had joined. He
would soon discover that living with one's frailties can bring you to
the brink of a new acceptance—not by skirting personal catastrophe,
but rather by plunging headlong into it.

That, however, was yet to come.

When he arrived at Daybreak as the new pastor in 1986—he had
been there earlier, in an interim capacity, in 1985—he would have
been struck by the fact that such a sanctuary existed in the throbbing,
pulsating, greater Toronto region. But it does. Just off the longest road
in Canada, Highway 11 or Yonge Street, you can find a collection
of buildings with a Swiss chalet–type façade that houses a pottery
shop, the carpentry shop they affectionately call "The Woodery,"

a kitchen, a recreational room, various accommodations, and a chapel. The people who work here constitute a L'Arche community, and it is known throughout Canada and abroad as Daybreak.

Founded by Jean Vanier himself in 1969, and the oldest L'Arche home in North America, it comprises some 13 acres, 8 houses, an old barn, 36 core members (those who have disabilities), and 32 assistants, half of whom are from countries other than Canada.

Among the assistants in the early 1990s were Carolyn and Geoffrey Whitney-Brown, who with their three children lived at Daybreak. The Whitney-Browns, fresh from earning doctorates in English literature from Brown University, experienced missioners in Africa, disciples of Ignatian spirituality at St. Beuno's in Wales, and creative intellectual and spiritual itinerants, were in many ways ideally suited to spend time at Daybreak. They brought with them a wealth of experience, energy, and focus. They would become Henri's friends. Carolyn, in particular, would play a key role in later years as an interpreter of the Nouwen legacy.

When I visualize Henri, I picture a burst of enthusiasm. I mean, Henri was often tormented, often lonely, and often needy, but my predominant impression was of someone very gifted at living generously in community. I visualize him bursting through the door of our kitchen with a vast bouquet of flowers for my birthday. I visualize him dancing at community parties, and believe me when I say that he was not a graceful man physically. He was awkward, tall, gangly, and would dance by leaping up and down—just bounding about.

I remember him laying out a beautiful Easter celebration with bright cloths and flowers, and encouraging other people to do likewise. I don't mean to imply that he did these things himself; because others knew that beauty mattered to him, they gladly joined in. He had an artistic temperament, and knew that he could engage people's senses through beauty. Arrangements mattered; color mattered; symmetry mattered.

And he was as colorful as his arrangements.

But even in this welcoming, warm, and hospitable atmosphere, shadows could be glimpsed. After all, Daybreak is a community of both the luminous and the eclipsed, the whole and the broken, the saint and the sinner. Carolyn Whitney-Brown saw Nouwen's presence as being as innovative as it was therapeutic:

> Henri was restless at L'Arche and wanted a bigger world, but he still fit into the L'Arche model and concept. It was no surprise that he quickly identified with the wounded, as he was wounded and handicapped himself. He craved affirmation, the knowledge that he was loved for *who* he was and not for what he *did*, not for what he *wrote*. Daybreak offered him an unconditional love that he would have found nowhere else.

Although Daybreak was in some sense a smaller world than that of Yale or Harvard, in other ways it was not. In one way, he left the hothouse of Harvard with its rivalries, conflicting personalities, and repressed emotions to come to Daybreak, a different but no less intense hothouse of feelings and needs. Nevertheless, Daybreak proved to be more freeing on several fronts. For instance, Henri could travel at any time of the year without the obstacles of curricular and committee meetings, he could accept as many speaking invitations as he liked, and he was not held back by the knowledge that he had an academic reputation to maintain.

> He experimented with taking core members of Daybreak with him, which nobody among the people at L'Arche who gave such public talks had really done before—at least on the same scale as Henri.

Nouwen stretched Daybreak as much as it stretched him; it could no more confine him than any other place he had called home, but its demands were different, the level of emotional honesty and transparency far more relentless than anything he had previously known. It's where the wounded gather. Carolyn Whitney-Brown:

> Henri says that some people try so hard to have no sins that they end up with no virtues either. You have to take the whole package

we call life; you have to live with the whole thing. So, when he came to Daybreak, he actually got a chance to live that "whole thing" in a much more concrete way. He lived with people—the intellectually disabled and the assistants—as one community. He lived intimately and not at a distance, and he knew that we were *all* handicapped, that it wasn't a simple division between the handicapped and the non-handicapped, and that we were all in various stages of wound-edness and immaturity. His extraordinary gift for intuition and his sacramental priesthood allowed him to see the community's brokenness at a more penetrative level than the rest of us did.

That gift for intuition helped to define his ministry as a priest. He was available to multitudes—his correspondents alone numbered in the thousands—and he brought his own vulnerability to those he counseled and to whom he administered sacramental absolution. Carolyn Whitney-Brown speaks candidly of her experience of confession with Nouwen, and in the process reveals the exquisitely liberating feeling of being sacramentally absolved:

Henri loved the sacrament of reconciliation; he loved auricular, personal confession. And he did because he was interested in the human mind and in the human heart, in human motivation. He was a psychologist after all, and understanding what it is that contributes to detracting from human growth into maturity commanded his professional interest and personal passion.

Having been raised a Protestant and later converting to Catholicism, this "confession thing" appealed to me. Because I had not been in any way obligated to go to confession prior to becoming Catholic, I found the experience freeing, a real pleasure. This is not, I discovered, the general experience among cradle Catholics. But for me going to confession was a joy.

So I would intermittently ask Henri if I could have a sacramental conversation. He would beam with pleasure, take out his calendar and flip back and forth, all the time getting more and more agitated as he complained over the many commitments he had made and how he wished he hadn't made them, and how much traveling he would have to do to honor these commitments. And then always, always, he would find a time in his calendar when he would be free, a calendar I came to see as miraculous because he would always find the time.

I would prepare myself for confession by thinking through every-thing that I was carrying heavily in community, my own anger, frustration, embarrassment, and shame. All the stuff you do before confession. I would go for a walk from my house to Henri's, past several buildings, beside a field, down a laneway all the way to the chapel, as he had a room above it. He'd greet me warmly and we would sit in his room, quietly at first, respectfully. And then I would start, usually with anger at my kids and all the petty resentments that came out of community, domestic and broader. I would talk about how community life at Daybreak gives you a lot of ways to hurt people and to get hurt. I would go deeper and deeper into my resentments, into their seething and controlling power and that would please Henri even more. In turn, that would compel me to start emptying out the icky psychic corners of my soul, turning my psychic pockets inside out and scraping out the lint for him. Then he would *really* get excited, and if there was a pause in my telling he would ask if that was all, inviting me to even greater disclosures. I would usually scrounge up a few things I wasn't sure whether to mention or not but figured I may as well. And then, when my part was over, he would take those giant hands of his and it looked as if he was holding all this stuff that I had just scraped out, that I wasn't happy about, and sometimes ashamed of, and he would say with utter sincerity: "That's wonderful!"

And now he would talk and speak of how all this stuff fit in with what I wanted from life, why I was doing what I was doing, what I yearned for as a human being, how I wanted to grow. He spoke about the way I noticed things, the way I saw things, and that if I remained unaware of these things I wouldn't be a human being. All this stuff that I thought was icky and repulsive, in his hands was turning into gold, into the kind of stuff that I could use to make me compassionate, or make me aware of what I need to do in the world and to live it bravely.

And then we would say a prayer; he would absolve and bless me and I would walk out of his room feeling like a walking sacrament, that I was a blessing to people around me. The people I encountered on my way to see Henri for confession, the very people who annoyed me and whom I scurried past because I didn't want to face them, now became for me a people transformed, shining with beauty.

And what is most important in all this is not that I had condemned anything, but that Henri had helped me to see that nothing was wasted, that every kind of human experience, every kind of person, everyone that makes up a community—none of this is wasted, it is all part of what we are trying to do in this world *as* human beings and not *despite* being human beings.

Nouwen was not frivolous about sin nor voyeuristic or gleeful about human failings. He understood the profound, aching need to be whole and he did not make light of the numerous stratagems and delusions that keep us protected from the sharp glare of truth. He grasped the healing and redemptive power of grace, the touch of God in the abyss of misery, the unfathomable capacity of love to shape the muck, mire, blood, and viscera of human experience into something beautiful.

Perhaps this was never more clear than in Nouwen's encounter with Adam Arnett.

Adam was my friend, my teacher, and my guide: an unusual friend, because he couldn't express affection and love in the way most people do; an unusual teacher, because he couldn't think reflectively or articulate ideas or concepts; an unusual guide, because he couldn't give me any concrete direction or advice. Adam was one of my housemates when I first came to L'Arche Daybreak....In and through Adam I came to a truly new understanding of those relationships of Jesus, not just as they were lived long ago, but as

Jesus desires us to live them now, with me and with us, through the weakest and most vulnerable people. Indeed, not only did I come to know more about God by caring for Adam, but also Adam helped me, by his life, to discover and rediscover the Spirit of Jesus alive in my own "poorness of spirit." Jesus lived long ago, but Adam lived in my time. Jesus was physically present to his disciples. Adam was physically present to me. Jesus was Emmanuel, God with us. Adam became for me a sacred person, a holy man, an image of the living God.[3]

Nathan Ball understood the significance of Adam for Nouwen earlier than Nouwen himself did:

Henri didn't always have the emotional flexibility to navigate multiple relationships in a fairly busy and fast-paced community, and there was also a tension between Henri's entrepreneurial can-do attitude and the kind of processes that are necessary to move a group of people, a community, forward *together*. Henri's larger-than-life mission and his engagement with the world and in the world was much broader than being simply present to the community at Daybreak. He was in and out, attracting a lot of attention, with TV studios, radio interviews, and carloads of people becoming an almost daily occurrence in our small urban oasis.

One important way of grounding him was Adam Arnett. When Henri arrived at Daybreak in 1986, Joe Egan, then director of the community, decided that if Henri was going to have the privilege of sharing life with people of disability, even if his mandate was going to be different from that of the regular assistants, nothing would be better than placing him in the home where Adam resided with others. Adam's home, then, became Henri's particular place of belonging in the community. He had his bedroom there, and he had his breakfast there, as well as several other meals with Adam, helped with his bathing, dressing, and eating, and he entered into his first intimate experience with someone with a disability. In fact, Adam had multiple disabilities, and Henri at first was perplexed and anxious about his obligations and capacity to rise to the challenges posed by Adam: he couldn't speak, depended on others when walking, couldn't feed himself or attend to other bodily needs. Henri was the exact opposite: a man of many words, a fast walker, impatient for the next thing. But as time went on, Henri, because of his insightful and inquisitive way, came to realize that Adam had an enormous amount to teach him, and that out of this emerging and maturing relationship he could come to discover, and the community with him, that his special gift was not as the practitioner but as the writer who could communicate the beauty that is Adam and the beauty that can be unearthed when one enters into a relationship with people with disabilities. Adam became his primary instructor and he became Henri's own icon of holiness, an *alter christus*, another Christ.

Henri's brilliance, in my perspective, found expression in a couple of ways. First: Henri was a man of remarkable compassion, and his healing presence could be found working in the lives of individuals as well as with groups. Second: his ability to communicate the dynamics of such compassion was extraordinary. Perhaps the best illustration I can provide is the way he coped with Adam's dying.

When Adam became ill and it was clear that he was dying, although Henri was out of the country, he quickly returned to Daybreak and became a font of compassion for Adam, his immediate family, the members of his house, and the Daybreak community itself. He would come daily to the hospital and infuse the place with a pastoral presence and care that was profoundly healing. His love, energy, and focus drew people together in a way that allowed them to see the sacredness of the moment; he provided a unity built on our ability to celebrate the gift of Adam's life even in the midst of a painful sadness.

Henri was the catalyst for this *quality* of caring and compassion that is, in my experience, very rare. I have been in hospitals and palliative care units many times, and I have close friends who are social workers, caregivers, teachers, and health professionals, and Henri's gift stands out by a large margin. His gift to the world in general, and in particular to the people who were in his life, was his ability to be a compassionate and transformative presence. His attending to Adam during his dying is the master expression of this gift.

He had written about compassion, mercy, generosity, and grace many times in his career, and although he had encountered moments that drew upon his personal reserves of compassion and empathy while in Latin America, while helping his close friends Jonas and Margaret cope with the tragic death of their daughter, Rebecca, and while helping his many friends experiencing personal crises, vocation upheaval, marital breakdown, and spiritual despair, the death of his beloved Adam brought a noble fruition to his anguished pursuit of the epitome of unconditional love in his life. He had become the amanuensis to a living document, inarticulate, awkward, flailing, and fractured, that managed to communicate with an ineffable beauty the love that eluded him all his life.

But just as he was wrestling with the challenges posed by Adam, he was also in the throes of a traumatic unwinding of his own life, his certainties, the very Ground of his spiritual life, and it was happening not at the intellectual level—which he could manage adroitly—but at the affective level, which he had enormous difficulty negotiating. Nathan Ball explains:

> Henri's intensity, his desire to know you and to relate to you, overrode the normal process by which people determine and manage their relationships. His overwhelming need to connect at the level of the heart bypassed the normal process, and people would often back away or receive confusing messages. The very gift that allowed him to connect with people during a time of acute crisis—his depth of compassion—was an obstacle when it came to mapping relationships during the time when things are normal. His inability to distinguish between a crisis situation and ordinary life when it came to modulating his approach meant that no matter the context or person, the classic Nouwen intensity was the defining feature. And this proved to be one of his particular handicaps while living in a community that struggled to accept and honor and not roman-

ticize the limitations and disabilities that we all have—external or internal. It takes a lot of commitment to stay present to the promise and hope of a community that believes that buried in the very heart of another's weakness is a gift for others.

Eager to be of service to others and puzzled by the tentativeness many had when entering into a relationship with him—at least on the terms he saw as normative—Nouwen once again expressed to his close friends his misgivings, feelings of failure, and sense of inadequacy. Orthodox priest and Notre Dame friend John Garvey, in a letter dated December 10, 1987, sought to assuage Nouwen's anxieties so early in his new ministry:

> You said that a lot of the people you work with are young, and form their own community, and don't need you as you would like to be needed. Something to remember about young people is that they still have a lot to learn about the impermanence of communities, which now seem very solid, even everlasting, to them. One thing that might separate you from them is the simple fact that you know more, and have experienced more, of separation and impermanence, and it is a reality they do not yet know as you know it. What you experience as a lack might be a real knowledge—not a cheery one, but true, and one they will have to learn in the long run.

Although what Garvey writes is both wise and a consolation—Nouwen's more adult appreciation of the evanescence of community making and the emotional minefields of nostalgia and youthful idealism nicely positioned him as pastor to Daybreak—he could not have fully understood the whirlpool of conflicting tensions and emotional torment that would very soon bring his friend and mentor to the brink of a breakdown.

Nathan Ball outlines the relentless crescendo that brings Nouwen to a new and pitiless darkness:

> When I look back at Henri's introduction to L'Arche and the inner motivation that he had, which was to find a new way of teaching and preaching outside of the conventional circuit, I realize that another,

perhaps unspecified, need was to find a home for his restless heart. And he did find that home in the context of the family quality of community at Daybreak.

But he was Henri. When he landed here, he jumped into the very deep end of the swimming pool, and he wasn't a good swimmer, couldn't tread water, in fact. This was a dangerous situation, but he was so determined to be in that pool that he created a problematical situation for us all. His desire to be in this new context of complicated relationships, and to do so immediately, without tempering, meant that very quickly this new and very foreign environment served to trigger several sets of circumstances that brought him to a place of very deep personal poverty, that brought him to a place of breakdown.

The "triggers" comprised his unresolved internal struggle with his sexual identity and the potential public implications associated with that awareness, his emotional dependency on the affirmation of others, the silence of God, his rootlessness, and his ever-diminishing sense of personal worth. But the key trigger, as it were, was his relationship with Nathan Ball.

Nouwen had met Ball first when they were together at Vanier's home in Trosly in 1985, and then they both arrived at Daybreak, via different routes but with the same fidelity to the L'Arche mission.

It is clear that his emotional attachment to Ball was all-consuming, that Ball was unsettled by the intensity of its expression, that the kind of reciprocity Nouwen expected could not happen. Ball felt increasingly compromised by Nouwen's possessiveness and neediness, and a strategy of distancing had to be deployed in the interests of community harmony and Ball's own psychological equilibrium. The effects of this distancing from the center of Nouwen's emotional stability, as he at one point described Ball, meant that he was now on the fast track to a psychic collapse.

Although it is true that the "spiritual friendship" between Ball and Nouwen was authentic and proved to be long lasting, at the core of the breakdown was Nouwen's inability to make peace with his own body—physical, sexual, and contingent. As Ball observes:

> Henri's dream, idealized hope, to come to a place where his longing to be at peace with himself—his intellectual passions, his life energies, his sexual struggles could be harmonized—was never realized; although he achieved a measure of resolution at Daybreak, he did not at any other juncture of his life journey.

> I am reminded of a powerful comment made by his father—who was already in his nineties at the time—remarking that almost from the moment of birth there was a restless and almost inconsolable dimension to Henri's life that really became the enduring theme of his life's work.

The quintessential problem then became Nouwen's sexual identity in terms of his public persona, an identity in great part shaped by his Dutch clerical formation. Ball sees two dimensions to the issue:

> Henri grew up in a cultural and ecclesiastical context in which the repression of sexuality had been normalized. That is the way he was socialized, irrespective of his own sexuality, gay or straight, and when he became a Roman Catholic priest, it took on added significance.

> From the very outset, Henri was clear that everything had to be subsumed under his vocation to proclaim the Gospel, to use his particular gifts to help people connect in a healing way with their suffering and the suffering of the world. He was insistent that his own struggles at the affective level needed to be put within the context of his evangelical mission. They needed to be subordinated to the higher calling.

> Now, there were people in the gay community who felt that the most important contribution he could make would be to become more public as a gay priest, given his prominence, credibility, and influence. He was tempted to do this, because he felt that the more public he was about his own sexual orientation and his personal struggles to remain faithful to his priestly vows, the greater the

possibility for personal healing. But he was also very much aware that in doing so, he risked politicizing his ministry and compromising his commitment to a universal and not selective audience. He lived with this enormous tension and did achieve something of a resolution following his breakdown.

But only *something* of a resolution. To the mind of his old colleague Richard Sipe:

Henri could not find what he called the mystical dimension of sexuality. It eluded him. Although Henri was homosexual in orientation, it very seldom affected his interaction with people. In his mind, his struggles around sexuality were private, and although we had many exchanges over the years, his sexuality rarely arose. He did once ask me some pointed questions about the nature of homosexuality: was it genetic, how did it develop, was it mutable, and how did it fit in with the spiritual life? And there was one other occasion when the issue arose between us, and that is when I asked him if he would write the introduction to my book *Sex, Priests and Power: The Anatomy of a Crisis*. He declined, and it was very rare of him to decline any request of mine. He was always generous and obliging. But this time the answer was a definitive "no." He was, in my view, a largely integrated person: he was honest and faithful to his canonical promises of chastity and celibacy, but I must say at great, great personal price to him. His sexual orientation remained unfinished business that he took to the grave with him.

But, as Sipe had previously averred, Nouwen was not the only prominent Catholic clerical celebrity of the last century who struggled with sexual integration. Thomas Merton, only a couple of years before his own unexpected death in Bangkok in 1968, found himself emotionally and spiritually roiled because of his love affair with M, a young nurse in Louisville. Merton was, of course, Nouwen's spiritual and literary mentor. As Sipe sees it, there was a striking if discrete parallel between Nouwen and Merton on the matter of mature, adult love that was late in the arriving. It is important to understand it if one is to get a complete picture of these two distinctly different but nonetheless connected spiritual masters of the twentieth century:

> After more than a quarter century of priestly life, both Merton and then Nouwen fell in love. Merton falls head over heels in love with a young nurse and really behaves, as so many of his friends and fellow monks have written, like a silly adolescent. He goes around hiding in offices and exploiting his friends, making them angry because of the manner in which he is using them to advance his own needs. Nouwen for the first time allows himself the human feelings associated with falling in love, in his case with another man, as befits his orientation. In both cases, their respective falling in love brought to the fore in quite dramatic ways the unfinished business that each needed to address.

Merton was by far the more successful in using his 1966 "episode of love" to examine his inadequacies, chart a way out of his dilemma, draw spiritual succor from his personal crisis, mine the good that his falling in love revealed about his personal capacity to love another, and explore the interlacing of the erotic with the agapaic. He had come to understand that a theology that has a platonic thrust to it, that prefers abstraction to incarnated reality, that harbors a deep, if covert, loathing of the body, is a theology, a spirituality stamped with the mark of a narrow and constricted rationality. A disembodied love is a partial love, etherealized, safe, but without that plenitude that distinguishes true, generous, and full love from its pale approximation.

Merton's capacity for love, limited as it was to the platonic and otherworldly, had prevented him from achieving that level of psychosexual maturation essential for a fully integrated spirituality. A flourishing spirituality demands a place for the body; a truncated spirituality depends on the body's segregation.

Merton wrote extensively about his love for M: detailed chronicling to be found in his "restricted journal" (he made it clear that his intention was that this journal, like all his other restricted journals, should eventually be published, but only twenty-five years following his death); the eighteen love poems that initially received a limited circulation; a document titled "Retrospect"; and a 23,000-word diary that he wrote in a week and called "A Midsummer Diary for M."

The diary is a hybrid and reflects the many pressures—interior and exterior—that Merton felt at work on his life. Part journal, part confession, part apologia, and part love letter, it is paradoxically both translucent and opaque, direct and convoluted, self-referential and other-oriented. There is a great deal of discussion of the French existentialist novelist and philosopher Albert Camus, of the absurd, of false solitude, of the "tyranny of diagnosis," of the fine distinction between *realizing* and *knowing*, and of the role of lucidity and compassion in human affairs. But it is really about his troubled soul, the Gordian knot that is his relationship with M, the need to bring irresolution to an end, to decide on a course of action that involves not only his "salvation" but that of M as well.

There is no doubt that the prose entries and letters—the poems are an exception—written during the course of the affair/episode of the heart, expressing and exploring his love for M, were often marred by an inadequacy of language that is unexpected in a wordsmith of Merton's caliber. His prose suffered from a strained sentimentality, an easy reliance on clichéd phrasing, bathos, and self-evident rationalization. Merton's feelings for M were, however, genuine, and his agonizing efforts to make sense of his riven life were honest if confused. The resolution—his recommitment to his vows and recognition that his life as a monk took precedence over his love for M—was the result of a period of intense self-scrutiny and unrelenting pain.

Nouwen's episode of the heart was different in genesis and resolution. Unlike Merton, who immediately picked up his pen, Nouwen was put under the care of a two-person team in Winnipeg, where he would remain in intensive therapy for six months. What precipitated the breakdown was, in his own words,

> ...the sudden interruption of a friendship. Going to L'Arche and living with very vulnerable people, I had gradually let go of my

inner guards and opened my heart more fully to others. Among my many friends, one had been able to touch me in a way I had never been touched before. Our friendship encouraged me to allow myself to be loved and cared for with greater trust and confidence. It was a totally new experience for me, and it brought me immense joy and peace. It seemed as if a door of my interior life had been opened, a door that had been locked during my youth and most of my adult life.

But this deeply satisfying friendship became the road to my anguish, because soon I discovered that the enormous space that had been opened for me could not be filled by the one who had opened it. I became possessive, needy, and dependent, and when the friendship finally had to be interrupted, I fell apart. I felt abandoned, rejected, and betrayed.[4]

Nouwen wrote this passage in his "secret journal," as he called it, a work that would be published eight years after its composition under the title *The Inner Voice of Love: A Journey through Anguish to Freedom*. After emerging from his Winnipeg sojourn and now returned to his Daybreak home, Nouwen explored the possibility of going public with his breakdown and with the journal he kept during his recovery. But he was uncertain of the wisdom of what could be seen as the too-hasty publication of something so raw. Naturally, he sought advice, as this letter to Jean Vanier of January 5, 1989, demonstrates:

Enclosed I am sending you a manuscript I wrote during my stay in Winnipeg. As you can see, these are reflections that were a direct fruit of the spiritual direction I received there. They are very personal, very direct, and very "raw." I have shared them with a few friends and the response has been quite intense. Some people feel strongly that this is the best book I have ever written. Others feel that I would make a great mistake by publishing it.

Unsure where to go, Nouwen outlined some of the arguments and personalities making the case for its imminent publication.

However, he wavered when faced by those who opposed such a decision, namely, Sue Mosteller, who presciently made the case that the text would assist him in writing other books but should not be published in its current form. Richard White cautioned that Nouwen was too much of a novice when it came to broken relationships and too inclined to generalize. Nouwen sought Vanier's advice, informing him that he would not consider publication at any time without Nathan Ball's support.

In the end, the book does not see the light of day until 1996, the year of his death. Insightful, meditative, tightly written, the book consists of a series of "spiritual imperatives" that are drawn directly from his personal anguish, but for all that, they contrast sharply with Merton's approach, stark in their structure, pointedly lacking in any specificity, exhortative rather than explorative, oracular rather than tentative. The prose is bloodless and detached; there are no names, no agony or emotional trial named for what it is. The book is much more a compendium of enlightened nostrums than a searing record of his total darkness, of the "one long scream coming from a place I didn't know existed, a place full of demons."[5]

Nouwen's reluctance to draw his readers into the particularities of his spiritual and emotional nightmare is understandable at many levels: his obsessive caution in protecting others; his resistance to mining his own misery for the purpose of celebrity or ideology; and his dread of so personalizing the experience that the larger mission of proclaiming the Gospel would be sundered by autobiography. His rationalization for not enfleshing the record is clever and inadvertently disingenuous:

> You have been wounded in many ways. The more you open yourself to being healed, the more you will discover how deep your wounds are....Your search for true healing will be a suffering search....The great challenge is *living* your wounds through instead of *thinking* them through....You need to let your wounds go down into your

heart. Then you can live them through and discover that they will not destroy you. Your heart is greater than your wounds.[6]

Although he could draw upon his Winnipeg experience to frame his suffering, extrapolate to include the universal human condition, and make sense of his own pain as part of a larger therapeutic strategy, in the end, by eliminating the *dramatis personae*, he made *The Inner Voice of Love* a public work devoid of private disclosure—in other words, a safe autobiographical snippet of a life trajectory of anguish.

But if the book's dynamic stalls under its own labored discretion, there are some key insights that surface, the most important of which is the notion of the "first love" and how this love is neither displaced nor forgotten because of a particular love. In fact, the latter can be the gateway to the former. The "first love" is glimpsed, accessed, and made real in light of the beauty of human love:

The love that came to you in particular, concrete human friendships and that awakened your dormant desire to be completely and unconditionally loved was real and authentic. It does not have to be denied as dangerous and idolatrous. A love that comes to you through human beings is true, God-given love and needs to be celebrated as such. When human friendships prove to be unlivable because you demand that your friends love you in ways that are beyond human capacity, you do not have to deny the reality of the love you received. When you try to die to that love in order to find God's love, you are doing something God does not want. The task is not to die to life-giving relationships but to realize that the love you received in them is part of a greater love.

God has given you a beautiful self. There God dwells and loves you with the first love, which precedes all human love. You carry your own beautiful, deeply loved self in your heart. You can and must hold on to the truth of the love you were given and recognize that same love in others who see your goodness and love you.

So stop trying to die to the particular real love you have received. Be grateful for it and see it as what enabled you to open yourself to God's first love.[7]

The particular love is Nathan, and the anguish generated by Nouwen's attachment, infatuation, and utter dependency on him is the principal trigger that prompted Nouwen's emotional cataclysm. It would be reductionist to conclude that Nouwen's breakdown was the result of suppressed homoerotic feelings, that the sublimation mechanism successfully employed in the past failed to work this time, and that the exclusive demands of such a love—unreciprocated by the loved one on the terms desired—was *the* defining feature of the relationship. The sexual dimension, no matter how disguised, was part of the relationship, if only for Nouwen and not for Ball. However, what both shared was an understanding of God's role in human love. Ball situates the episode of love, the Winnipeg recovery, and Nouwen's re-insertion into the Daybreak community dynamic:

> After his breakdown, Henri had what I would call a re-conversion. He plumbed to a deeper level in terms of self-understanding and in terms of how he would live the kind of life he believed God called him to live. In order to better navigate his own relational and affective seas, he needed to better anchor himself in God. By doing so, he felt, to mix my metaphors, that this more profound grounding in God enabled him better to face the wild currents that could so easily toss him about.

> He needed to hold on to God in order to weather the affective tos and fros of his life, the multiple pressures and voices clamoring for his support or endorsement, and in order for that to happen he needed to make what he called "the second yes," a spiritual recon-version, a more substantive penetration of the Divine will.

There is no doubt that Nouwen's breakdown was a matter of an ever-accumulating and unaddressed series of pressure points, that his depression was not the result of one factor alone, and that he had yet to appropriate as his own the liberating truth so eloquently captured

in Daniel O'Leary's phrasing: "We are treasured beyond measure by a mercy that does not depend on our worthiness—that carries no inspection for perfection."[8]

Nouwen had still to make peace with his body—the human body. He needed to reject the residue of a dangerous angelism, the vestigial marks of Jansenism, his perduring detestation of and embarrassment over his physical awkwardness.

Then, in April of 1991, the circus came to town.

Although Nouwen had been fascinated by the circus since childhood, and the image of the clown was deployed by him in an earlier book—*Clowning in Rome: Reflections on Solitude, Celibacy, Prayer and Contemplation* (1979)—it was his encounter with the trapeze act of the Flying Rodleighs at the Circus Barum in Freiburg, Germany in April of 1991 that proved to be formative in many new and startling ways. Rodleigh Stevens, the founder of the flying trapeze team, remembers the details of his first puzzling meeting with a man who would prove to have a life-transforming effect on the artists:

> We were performing in Freiburg with the German Circus Barum, and Henri was in town meeting with his German publicists, helping them translate one of his books into German. His father was with him at the time and they decided to take in one of our performances.
>
> Henri was enthralled with what he saw and was determined to make a connection with us. He asked the circus director right after our performance if he could meet with us, and as you can appreciate, a meeting right after a performance is not an ideal time, especially as we were preparing for the next act.
>
> As chance would have it, my sister was buying some candy for her daughter when she was seen by Henri and immediately approached by him. She invited him to meet with us, he did so, attended the next performance and thus began a creative and spiritual relationship that lasted up to the time of his death.

Nouwen was so taken by the team, their artistry, their unabashed physicality, that he not only befriended the Flying Rodleighs—and

Rodleigh Stevens in particular—he entered their lives, their thoughts, and their dreams. He became part of them. He would blitz them with his questions, insert himself into their pre- and post-performance discussions, listen intently to the exchanges between Stevens and the rest of the team, and participate in their post-mortem reflections.

Not surprisingly, at first they were wary of this importunate, ungainly gentleman, keen on engaging them at every moment about their art and doing so in their face. But he quickly won them round with his transparency, animated personality, and social awkwardness. They came to love him.

He began to interview the members of the troupe with the intention of writing a book—a work of fiction—that resulted in several drafts of chapters and transcriptions but was never completed. He would write in a letter to the Rodleighs dated May 14, 1991, that

> [I] see in your life many images that can help me understand and explore the meaning of the life of the spirit. Flying, catching, trusting and daring, discipline and cooperation, care for one another and listening to one another, all are part not only of your life, but also of the life of the spirit that I am writing about.[9]

Although his attraction to the Flying Rodleighs was in part predicated on his falling in love with a new conceit, with an extended metaphor for the spiritual life, Nouwen's seduction was both more complicated and simple than any of his rationalizations would allow. Stevens explains:

> I think Henri really tried to identify with us but from a different level, as it were. It was his brother Laurent who said to me that Henri is trying to live *through* your body with his body and that he is not at all comfortable being a tall, gangly, six-foot priest. He wanted to be an athlete and he realized his childhood dreams of swinging on a trapeze vicariously by being part of our team. He did this by getting into our heads, getting into our souls, getting into our stories, our lives—and this was the way he could feel like that

person on the flying trapeze without actually having the physical experience himself.

At one point, actually, we contrived to give him that physical experience and we positioned him on the trapeze, held up by myself, secured by the safety lines, with a swing and then a drop to the net. After he landed in the net, he lay there for three minutes with this enormous smile on his face. He just lay in the net, mute, immobile, totally silent, just the big grin. Adrenaline had taken over his whole body; he was frozen in the moment. Finally, he turned slowly to us and said, "That was wonderful!" And it was—both for him and for us witnessing the pleasure and peace it brought him.

What the Flying Rodleighs meant to Nouwen was community, aesthetic and spiritual marriage, and the celebration of the body *qua* body. Stevens saw and appreciated what that meant for Nouwen:

> We were therapy for Henri. He would come and stay with us, and every time he left he was relaxed and a lot more jovial than when he arrived. But it worked both ways. Because he was a comic with a delicious sense of humor, he made us laugh as well, although there were a few occasions when we laughed both with him and at him. He could be quite the klutz.

It wasn't only humor that they shared, however, it was community. Humor was the adhesive. Nouwen's need for community never abated, and he sought it in the most exotic and marginal of places. With the Daybreak community, he functioned as pastor as well as co-worker, but with the Flying Rodleighs it was different in kind. Religion never entered into the arena of their shared lives; he never preached or exhorted; his compassionate attention to their private lives was not ministerial; he entered fully into the nexus of their lives, their counselor, their friend, and their ardent admirer. When he died, they were stricken. Stevens recalls:

> He knew us from the inside out; he was the *only* person who was part of our team who never performed with us. And when we first heard the news that he had died, we dedicated our very first

performance to his memory. It was a very poignant moment, and when we all gathered backstage after the performance, we were at first silent and then we all looked at each other and agreed aloud how very tough that show was to do.

Nouwen had a profoundly spiritual impact on the Flying Rodleighs, although they were at first disinclined as a group to see it that way. He wanted to help them see that what they did was more than entertainment, more than earning a living: they were creating a community. To assist them to better understand that, Nouwen would gently but persistently prod them into reflecting as much on the *why* as the *how* of their art. Especially with the more dramatic high-wire acts, he would ask them outright:

> How do you manage to focus so completely on your act when you have so many distractions? Your mind is given over to travel plans, schedules, personal hardships, minor body injuries, and the worries created by unresolved personal issues. But because your work is so demanding, requiring full concentration, otherwise the consequences could be deadly, you have to put everything aside for the ten minutes of your act.

He tried to show his teammates that those ten minutes constituted a form of prayer, that when you let everything go, you rest in God.

Stevens was convinced that in helping them understand their artistry, more specifically the acts that required unconditional and integrated group work, Nouwen came to better see his own prayer life as something that required community, trust, and the utter abandonment that comes with placing your life in God's hands.

In other words, the Flying Rodleighs allowed him to see his life as that of a *Jongleur de Dieu*, a Tumbler or Juggler for God. Although a medieval conceit—linked with the courtly love tradition and the troubadours—the *jongleur* had a special, subversive, and beatific function to perform. The English essayist, poet, and popular theologian Gilbert Keith Chesterton brilliantly encapsulates the revolutionary spiritual heroism of the *jongleur* when he writes in his biography of St. Francis of Assisi:

> Francis, at the time or somewhere about the time when he disappeared into the prison or the dark cavern, underwent a reversal of a certain psychological kind; which was really like the reversal of a complete somersault, in that by coming full circle it came back, or apparently came back, to the same grotesque posture. It is necessary to use the grotesque simile of an acrobatic antic, because there is hardly any other figure that will make the fact clear. But in the inward sense, it was a profound spiritual revolution. The man who went into the cave was not the man who came out again; in that sense he was almost as different as if he were dead, as if he were a ghost or a blessed spirit. And the effects of this on his attitude towards the actual world were really as extravagant as any parallel can make them.[10]

There are obvious similarities between Francis and Nouwen: their physical angularity; their single-minded devotion to the Gospel; their artistic temperament; their loyalty to ecclesial superiors; and their personal anguish. When Francis emerged from his prison/cavern a different person—transformed to some degree by his liminal experience—Nouwen could be said to have experienced something similar in his "dark moment" in Winnipeg. He came out of it changed, not as radically, perhaps, as the Franciscan hagiographers would have us understand was the case with Francis, but significant enough to be different. The aptness of the tumbler metaphor can be seen against the backdrop of Nouwen's enhanced attention to the body, not as something to be feared, suppressed, scrutinized, and neutered, but as something that can be seen as a channel of grace, the means by which through discipline, tenderness, trust, and human interdependence, the body-in-performance, the body-in-act, is like prayer, *is* prayer.

If the Flying Rodleighs provided Nouwen with a liberating insight into how the somatic and spiritual work in tandem, Nouwen provided them, specifically Stevens, with that unique combination of compassion and empathy, that ability to read the living document in front of him, that was by now the signature feature of his pastoral style.

In a moving tribute to this personal quality, Stevens outlines the last time they met, just two months before Nouwen's death:

> It was July of 1996 and we met in a town close to Frankfurt. He was a bit distracted, anxious about his trip to St. Petersburg for the documentary to be shot at the Hermitage and based on his book on the Rembrandt painting.
>
> We spoke about my wife's pregnancy and the requirement of the German government that she have an amniocentesis due to her age. Henri was very concerned about this development and pressed us on what we would do if the test revealed any fetal abnormalities. My wife and I were horrified that he would think we would abort because of some identified defect, but then we realized that just as we were reflecting on the sometimes torturous road of parenting, he was in the process of parenting *us*.
>
> As it happened, the test was negative and we were spared the anguish but there is no way we would not have had our son. Birth defects or not, we would have loved him. Unfortunately, Henri did not live long enough to see our son, Bradley, born three months after Henri's death. Among our many memories of Henri, whose fame, by the way, we only came to realize at his funeral, as he was always very self-effacing with us, was that this overriding concern for the unborn Bradley spoke eloquently to his abiding belief in the utter sacredness of life.

It is hardly surprising that Nouwen would be solicitous, intentional, even aggressive when faced with any threat, real or notional, to the holiness of all life—broken and whole. After all, Adam Arnett, disfigured, incapacitated, and wholly dependent on others, was for him a vehicle of grace, an embodiment of God's beauty, and a living sacrament of love.

Constitutive of this love is trust, the trust he saw amply displayed by the Flying Rodleighs, a trust that he continued to find absent in his

own life. Although he repeatedly asked his siblings and his parents if they loved him and received confirmation of their love, he remained emotionally unpersuaded. This was especially true of his father. Laurent Nouwen speaks frankly of Henri's efforts to wrest from his father a final blessing, a public sign of his approval:

> After my mother died, Henri approached my father on many occasions and in many ways to get more intimate, culminating some fifteen years after her death with a moment of mutual forgiveness in a monastery in the south of Belgium.
>
> They were very different personalities and in competition with each other. Henri was desperate to elicit from our father an ultimate blessing acknowledging that he, Henri, was good in himself and worthy of love. But my father was not sure what was being asked of him, and given that he would have related to his father in a similar manner, it was not in him to do what Henri needed. And so Henri had to go beyond our father to another Father.

The search for this other Father would occupy Nouwen for years and would result in a book that many consider his masterpiece: *The Return of the Prodigal Son: A Story of Homecoming*. Not insignificantly, he would dedicate the book to his father for his ninetieth birthday.

A sustained and imaginative meditation on Rembrandt's *Return of the Prodigal Son*, the book incorporates the salient themes of Nouwen's spirituality: hospitality, forgiveness, unconditional love, *kenosis*, first love, woundedness, the role of the visual arts and beauty in the quest for God, the relationship of father with son, and prophetic vision. Transfixed by the seventeenth-century Dutch painter's exquisite painting of the younger son kneeling in front of his father, with others, including the elder son, in the background, Nouwen was compelled by Rembrandt's evocation of paternal love's divine tenderness of heart to investigate the layers of meaning to be found in St. Luke's parable of human and divine prodigality, to mine the riches of the painter's own spiritual journey, to probe deeper into his own cautious and truncated inner life.

The book not only draws on some of the best commentary on Rembrandt and his art, pertinent exegetical studies, and relevant events from the author's own life, it creates a portrait of a "homecoming" that is *both* profoundly individual in its particular details at the same time as it is universal in its anthropology and psychology.

The parable of the Prodigal Son in the Gospel of Luke, upon which the painting is based, can be read at various levels, and biblical scholars, homilists, and spiritual writers have been doing that for centuries.

The younger son of the parable asks for his inheritance from his father, which he then goes and quickly squanders. Reduced to penury and starving, he determines to return home to seek shelter and survival; after all, he reasons, at least he won't be turned away and he'll have a roof over his head. Alerted that his wayward son is on his way back home, the father runs to meet him; the father rejoices in his heart, welcomes his son, and then orders the fatted calf to be slaughtered. (Luke 15:22-24) The elder son—ever-dutiful, reliable, sturdy, and committed to the estate—is appalled by his father's unchecked delight in his brother's return. The resentment of the elder son is juxtaposed with the relief and gratitude of the younger son and the unalloyed joy of the father.

Christians have traditionally understood this parable in terms of the stark contrasts that it offers regarding the brothers and their respective response to their father's unconditional love. Nouwen, overwhelmed by the Rembrandt painting and the centrality he accords the father figure, uses the parable to reveal how each reader/viewer must see *each* of the key principals through the lens of their lived experience. During the period when he was sequestered in Winnipeg undergoing therapy and struggling to make sense of his dark night, he writes:

> ...the few books I could take with me were all about Rembrandt and the parable of the prodigal son. While living in a rather isolated place, far away from my friends and community, I found great

consolation in reading the tormented life of the great Dutch painter and learning more about the agonizing journey that ultimately had enabled him to paint this magnificent work.[11]

Conceived at the heart of agony and out of a long gestation, *The Return of the Prodigal Son* emerged from a labor of spiritual passion and ardent desire. At the same time, it was a form of exorcism. Although all his personal demons were not expelled—many were stilled only—Nouwen had achieved a degree of distance and insight that is remarkable for its focus and detail. With both Rembrandt and Luke as his guides Nouwen probed the multivalent potentialities for mystery and understanding in the painting/parable, inserted himself into the visual and theological drama being played out in image and word, and sought that consummation devoutly to be wished: reconciliation with his father.

Nouwen himself acknowledged the personal connection:

When I saw the poster of the Rembrandt painting with the returning son being embraced by his father, I was totally overwhelmed and I said, "That's where I want to be." I began to think of myself as the runaway son wanting to return home. But then...the older son suddenly started to speak to me. I am the oldest son myself and I recognized a lot of resentment in me, a lot of not fully enjoying where I was in my life. I woke up to the truth that *both* those young people [the two brothers] *lived* in me....One member of my community [Daybreak] said "Henri, you're always talking about yourself being the prodigal son, and you're often talking about yourself being the elder son, but now it's time for you to become the father! That's who you're called to be."[12]

The community member who spoke so insightfully to him was Sister Sue Mosteller, who, more than most, understood the complex interplay of idea and emotion, personal biography and gospel narrative, vocation and profession that played out in Nouwen's life as he struggled to discipline the fears that drove them, to make those fears subservient to a higher good. Mosteller saw in the post-Winnipeg

Nouwen, the Prodigal Son Nouwen, an introspective and wise writer who grasped the centrifugal forces that hobbled him:

> Henri spoke about the first loneliness, by which he meant the reason for his coming to Daybreak, the loneliness of a bachelor professor, of a celibate priest, aching for warm relationships. But then, after the first year he realized that there is another passage, another movement, he has to go through. And so from L'Arche he goes to Winnipeg and experiences a far more intense loneliness, the second loneliness. This is much more profound than the first—now he must face his relationship with God, accept his particular suffering, and stand in that, live in that.

> Loneliness brings him to L'Arche and L'Arche brings him to loneliness. It is all one movement. But then there is a parallel movement, but reverse. Aware and appreciative of what he calls the second love, the love that is grounded in the family, in intimate relationships, in friendships, he comes to realize, after Winnipeg, that the limitations and deficiencies of this love bring us to what he calls the first love. This love is God's unconditional, unrestricted, and all-encompassing love; we are all the daughters and sons of God; we are God's beloved.

The first love fills in the weaknesses and inadequacies of the second love, but for Nouwen, the route to the Father is through the father; to fully appropriate the truth of the first love, he must come to a deeper valuing of the second. And in this case, and not for the first time, a mirror becomes the agent for an epiphany:

> …on looking into a mirror, I was struck by how much I look like my dad. Looking at my own features, I suddenly saw the man whom I had seen when I was twenty-seven years old: the man I had admired as well as criticized, loved as well as feared. Much of my energy had been invested in finding my own self in the face of this person, and many of my questions about who I was and who I was to become had been shaped by being the son of this man. As I suddenly saw this man appearing in the mirror, I was overcome with the aware-

ness that all the differences I had been aware of during my lifetime seemed so small compared with the similarities. As with a shock, I was indeed heir, successor, the one who is admired, feared, praised, and misunderstood by others, as my dad was by me.[13]

Nouwen's genius can be found in his describing, as if for the first time, an experience that is singular, when what he is doing is taking an experience that is universal and mining it for the biographical nuggets, the personal narrative, that gives the insight a recognizable but still unique hue. Although at some point every man will see himself in his father, recognize that the father is in the son and the son in the father, for Nouwen the drama of this relationship is played out more extravagantly, the stakes markedly higher, the personal emotional investment more costly.

In *The Return of the Prodigal Son*, Nouwen was able to achieve what had eluded him for so long: a new compact with his father, in great measure mediated by the leveling experience of the Winnipeg breakdown and enabled by his reading of the painter Rembrandt's own spiritual anguish. He wanted to make his peace with his father— had for some time—not necessarily because he had intimations of an imminent death but because an earlier experience, recorded in *Beyond the Mirror: Reflections on Death and Life* (1992), allowed him a taste of the love that beckoned but could not be savored.

On a walk with one of the core members of the Daybreak community, he was struck by the mirror of a passing van, admitted to hospital, operated on, and found himself hovering on death:

> What I experienced then was something I had never experienced before: pure and unconditional love. Better still, what I experienced was an intensely personal presence, a presence that pushed all my fears aside and said, "Come, don't be afraid. I love you." A very gentle, non-judgmental presence: a presence that simply asked me to trust and trust completely.[14]

Nouwen survived his surgery and his wounds healed, but he couldn't help feeling disappointed that his foretaste, his presage of the new life proffered by death was simply that—an intimation. His being able to rest fully in the arms of God was merely a prod to live more deeply his life now. It was a Lazarus moment.

But it did illustrate—if somewhat overly dramatic in its expression and urgency—something of the constant preoccupation with death that was a leitmotif running through both his work and his life. In fact, his various works on death and dying—*In Memoriam* (1980); *A Letter of Consolation* (1982); *Our Greatest Gift: A Meditation on Dying and Caring* (1994)—provide evidence of his efforts to recreate for modern Christianity the medieval tradition of befriending one's death, the *ars moriendi*, the strategy of holy dying.

This is naturally in sharp contrast with our contemporary Western culture, which sanitizes the dying experience, marginalizes the dying person through isolation and sedation, evacuates the language of medicine of all raw and beautiful evocations and representations of death and substitutes a discourse of benign illusion, and frames death as extinction, cessation, a utilitarian's nightmare. Over the years, particularly following the death of his mother in 1978, the wrenching consequences of which occupied the grieving son for much of his life, Nouwen persevered with his efforts to situate dying within the context of loving, to deepen the experience of solidarity that defines palliative care at its best, to show the face of compassion *in extremis*:

> We can be healed from our fear of death, not by a miraculous event that prevents us from dying, but by the healing experience of being a brother or sister of all humans—past, present, and future—who share with us the fragility of our existence. In this experience, we can taste the joy of being human as a foretaste our communion with all people.[15]

It is by being present with the dying, our companions on the way, that we the living can find in their vulnerability, their fragility, our hope, our expansive capacity to love, our flawed and yet glorious humanity. Compassion is a two-way street.

Nouwen had been fearful of death because it marked the end of activity, because its finality meant that he could not improve his competitive advantage over many of his peers, that with death you have the definitive validation. Nothing else is possible. It also meant that the unresolved issue of his life would remain permanently unresolved: he would be unreconciled with his father.

His experience with the van, and the maturation of his thought around death as he worked with others processing their own death or grieving the loss of ones close to them, allowed Nouwen to grow more comfortable with his own mortality. He feared now not the loss of his gifts nor accomplishments, as he knew that true fruitfulness, lasting fecundity, comes after one's death. It was dying after the "big mistake" that concerned him, as he notes in the following June 30, 1996, entry of his diary. He is traveling with his father and they are watching a soccer game on television. He is moved by the picture of the defeated Czech goalkeeper following a competition with the German team for the European Cup, and muses on the depth of the player's dejection, his isolation by his own teammates following the defeat, and his inconsolable realization that in spite of his many previous successes, *this* is what he will be remembered for:

> After a long and fruitful life, one unhappy event, one mistake, one sin, one failure can be enough to create a lasting memory of defeat. For what will we be remembered? For our many acts of kindness, generosity, courage, and love, or for the one mistake we made toward the end?...Sometimes I think about dying before the great mistake![16]

It is possible that this anxious sentiment was free floating, but it could also speak to his trepidation that one false step, one imprudent moment or bad judgment, could bring his reputation down around his ears. It mattered to him still the reputation that he had meticulously cultivated for many decades; it is not a trifling thing; and it could go in the twinkling of an eye. But at the end of the diary entry, he reflects more philosophically on the transience of a reputation, the fickleness of human judgment, and the fact that only God knows us in our essence. There is deep consolation in this knowledge, and Nouwen is more serene than hysterical about the "big mistake" than he was when first ruminating on the personal desolation of the Czech goalkeeper.

In just a few months, none of this mattered. He would be dead.

The last days of Henri Nouwen are frantic, puzzling, quotidian, and wondrous—just like Nouwen himself. Invited to collaborate in the making of a film documentary on his Prodigal Son book, he returned from his sabbatical—the record of which would be posthumously published as *Sabbatical Journey: A Diary of His Final Year*—and prepared to go to St. Petersburg for the shoot at the Hermitage. He would break his trip by stopping off at Holland unaware—or perhaps at a subliminal level not so unaware—that this would be his last native homecoming.

Sue Mosteller recounts the last time she and Nathan Ball spent time with Nouwen just before his departure from Toronto:

> It was difficult at first finding some time, but we did. We had a Sunday together. After celebrating the Eucharist in a psychiatric ward with one of our people—it was a beautiful moment—we had a Mass that was very intimate and then we spent some time with her and had a drink. Afterwards we went to the CN Tower for breakfast and talked about Henri's return to Daybreak. He was adamant that he needed to reconnect, that he needed to be rooted, and to that end he would go back to his office. We argued against that and told him that if he did so he would be dead—the sheer minutiae and demands of administration would kill him. I don't think we were very successful in convincing him.
>
> And then we came down from the Tower, took the ferry to the Toronto Islands and walked for hours, returning to our car at the end of the day and then said goodbye—in the parking lot.

None of them could have known that it was their final parting involvingthe three of them. Nouwen left shortly after this and flew to Holland on his way to Russia. His brother Laurent recalls Henri's last visit to his native country:

> When Henri came to Holland, he was very exhausted and he had a pain in his chest. When he arrived at the airport, he was taken immediately to his hotel, where he suffered his first heart attack and then moved to a hospital. I remember that when they phoned to tell me this, I asked what was the first plane I could take to Canada to see him and was told that I didn't need to worry as he was resting in a hospital practically around the corner, as it were.

> All the family gathered as quickly as possible and we could see that he was going through a very difficult time, that he was struggling. We attended to him for a week, especially during the nights, and he did rally a bit. They decided to release him from intensive care as they figured he would survive. So, for the first time since his admittance, he spent the evening alone, and that is when he suffered the second and lethal attack. He died with no one around him.

> We received an early-morning call telling us what happened, and we immediately returned to the hospital, including my father. He was distraught and wept, saying that it should be him and not Henri who died. It was the deepest sadness for my father, who died a year later at ninety-four, a year of unrelieved sorrow and pain.

> I believe Henri had by this time truly made friends with death. In fact, he had done so earlier, when he nearly died from the van accident; my father was at his bedside *then*, too.

The co-founder of the Spirituality and Psychiatry section of Great Britain's Royal Society of Psychiatrists, the spiritual writer and psychiatrist Larry Culliford, sees Nouwen's death as full of irony, unanswered questions, unheeded warnings, and perhaps even hubris:

> I was struck by the tremendous, if rather tragic, irony of Henri's ill health and demise. For me, part of being spiritually minded includes taking good care of the temple of the body. I admit I can do better on this point myself, but Henri repeatedly notes an unusual degree of fatigue and fails, apparently, to seek medical advice over it. How

quickly a few tests would have revealed his narrowing coronary arteries, which could have been fixed surgically in no time.

Henri even spoke of a gathering he went to attended by a cardiologist and other medical people. I think it was one of the weddings in Europe at which he officiated. Why, I wonder, did he not mention his weariness to someone there and get it checked out? Astonishingly, too, he went reluctantly to the fitness club a few times, and also went on the trapeze apparatus, allowing himself to be held aloft then dropped into the safety net. It is just amazing that he did not have a heart attack there and then!

The irony, of course, as it seems to me, is that Henri wrote a lot about listening to discern God's will and intention without hearing the message that he seems to have been given repeatedly over that final year of his life. He seems to have been warned about his health and impending death in so many ways, but failed to interpret them accurately, preferring to think about his father's mortality, while continuing to wonder what he and various friends would be saying to each other in twenty years' time. Did he ever give a thought, I wonder, to Thomas Merton's sudden exit from life, for example? Or was this his final and fateful conceit, that he was somehow immortal. We'll never know![17]

Culliford's observation that Nouwen did not appear to give much thought—or at least published thought—to the bizarre and unexpected death of his mentor, Thomas Merton, might well suggest that as much as he thought about death, as much as he wrote about death, and as much as he blissfully welcomed its imminence at the time of his serious accident, he never planned for it, he never anticipated it, and he never employed the kind of prophylactic strategies that would have kept it at bay for some time to come. And when it did come, stealthily at night, it took him when he was alone, isolated, and unprepared. He had, after all, told many of his Canadian and American friends not to fly to Holland to see him, as he was on the mend and would be back soon. He was already using faxes and the telephone to tell them that he was cutting the trip short and would be home earlier than expected.

Because the people at Daybreak had no reason to suspect otherwise, they were all stunned by the news that he had died. Carolyn Whitney-Brown recalls it well:

> I remember very clearly that when we heard Henri had died, we were struck by a deep sense of marvel, that he was now on the most remarkable of journeys, and that his hunger for God was now being satisfied. This was the culmination of a graced life, and although we were beyond sad, we also experienced a deep peace throughout that day.
>
> The reality set in the next day, the knowledge that he had now left our community permanently, and our grieving, a deep grieving, began, but I think this grieving was about us as a community, about what Henri's death meant for us as a community.

Whitney-Brown believes that Nouwen "died at a point of equilibrium," and that Jesuit Bill Clarke's observation that Nouwen returned to his father and to his fatherland as the Prodigal Son and then died in their metaphoric embrace has the ring of truth about it and a mystical symmetry that is appealing. But she also notes that he seemed less than enthusiastic about making the trip itself, that he was tired, tired from his sabbatical (an indication perhaps that it was not much of a sabbatical), and that he felt his very recent return to Daybreak demanded more time for his settling in. Still, there was the agreement he had signed with Dutch producer Jan van den Bosch about the Rembrandt documentary, and he was keen on seeing the painting again at the Hermitage. The stage was set for the final act.

Daybreak prepared for his return—in a casket. His "first funeral" was in the Cathedral of Utrecht, with principal presider Cardinal Archbishop and Primate Adrianus Simonis. Vanier was the eulogist. He reminded the gathered of Nouwen's "prophetic vision," a term Nouwen defined as looking at people and this world through the eyes of God. It was a Blakean moment:

How are we going to live on without Henri? How are we going to be together as we feel the biting pain of his absence? Nobody can give answers to these questions but we must trust that together we will discover new life among us. In fact, it is already happening. Henri's funeral has brought together people who are not comfortable in each other's presence. Healing and reconciliation are opening in the open space that Henri has left behind. The open space of a prophetic vision where we are not only Christians but others who are searching for truth, searching for love, searching for a real spirituality, a spirituality that will flow from the broken hearts of people, not through power but through the wounded hearts of people. So we must fill this empty space.[18]

Vanier's recognition that the heart of Nouwen's spirituality was inclusive and not dogmatic or restrictive, that his calling for a way of seeing others *through* the eyes of God was not formulaic or the special reserve of the religious but the common inheritance of all, meant that filling in the empty space left by his departure was going to be a universal summons.

Back home, the people at Daybreak were preparing themselves for something more mundane: the building of his casket, the preparations for his "second funeral," and the processing of the experience so critical to a L'Arche community. Whitney-Brown sets the context and provides the narrative of his final homecoming:

Some while before he died, Henri had asked the woodworking shop at Daybreak to make his funeral casket for him. And so we did, not realizing we would need to do so at short notice. We had no previous experience with constructing coffins, so we built—with some good practical advice courtesy of our local funeral home—a broom closet, making sure that the bottom was stronger than normal, as you don't want the body falling through. And we made a nice lid, although it was really a door, and attached some handles so that in the end it looked like a respectable coffin.

The very day that Henri's body arrived, we wrote notes on the back of the lid, which of course only he would see. The director of our woodworking shop happened to be a former funeral home director, and so, with the compliance of the local funeral home, which happened to be very fond of L'Arche, we were able to take on a more active role than would ordinarily be permitted. We helped lay out Henri; we took his necktie off and rumpled his hair; we placed his favorite stole on him; we placed a triangular pillow under his torso, slightly elevating him so that people could touch him. Henri had been insistent that we should not be reticent about touching the physical remains of somebody, because although their heart, their spirit is now with God, there is still the physical body, and we should talk to the dead, pat their body, make tender, physical connection, and say goodbye.

The requiem itself was to be held in a large church—the Slovak Catholic Cathedral of the Transfiguration in Markham—and we went there and surrounded the church with vases and vases of sunflowers. The congregation was huge and it was diverse. There were people who had not come back to Daybreak for years who showed up; there were people who didn't get along with each other; there were military personnel, as Henri had given many retreats to the U.S. military; there were peace activists and committed pacifists. And there were celebrities, including the children's entertainment guru Mr. Rogers.

Children were in evidence everywhere, a dance troupe from Daybreak performed, and the prayers of the faithful were spoken by a vast number of his friends.

It rained from the time his body arrived in Richmond Hill from Holland, throughout the wake, and up to the time we arrived for the Mass. But by the time the funeral was over, the rain had stopped. The gravesite was gray and overcast, but no rain, and then just as we were walking to his home in the chapel building with his family, the sun came out and we had a most beautiful sunset. It was as if the weather conformed to the liturgical sequence. Beauty at the end.

The drama of his passing isn't exhausted by the sacred theatre of the obsequies, nor by the tributes paid, the tears wept, and the exhortations made to cling to his legacy, to let it ferment within the hearts and minds of his disciples. No, a good part of the drama is played out in the mystery of the life lived, the sometimes debilitating contradictions of his life, the extreme oscillations of emotion that characterized that life, and the fundamental paradox that in the end defined him: a person called to announce God's impartial and inclusive love, but who in his own life felt that love withheld; a person destined to address the wounds of others, but for a long period confounded by his own brokenness.

Although a professional psychologist, he never received the highest credential (the doctorate); although a professor at institutions of higher education distinguished by their pedigree, he was never quite of the club, churning out learned books and peer-reviewed articles; although a priest, he never managed to function in a conventional pastoral capacity, and all his various forays into exotic territories like missionary work and the cloister never managed to result in a long-term commitment and had about them the tinge of romanticism. In every aspect, Nouwen was a misfit. A holy misfit.

An endlessly curious person, Nouwen followed his interests whether they took him to an art gallery, into a circus tent, or into a community of and for those living with disabilities. He fit perfectly the definition of the *gyrovagus* or wandering monk. In its purest sense, this type of monk was a sign of decadence, spiritual laxity, and a threat to the vow of stability monks were obligated to make. But Nouwen, a wandering monk in the sense of a rootless contemplative trying his hand at various spiritual and pastoral undertakings, is perhaps a model or type of the contemporary post-modern Christian.

Readers and audiences across continents have devoured his books and consider themselves privileged to have heard him, whether in a church, university hall, auditorium, or television studio. There is something in the way Nouwen was Nouwen that had, and continues to have, wide appeal. In part, his own restlessness spoke to the restlessness of his contemporaries—he chronicled his disquiet and struggle for wholeness in ways that could entice others to reflect on their own respective situation rather than respond defensively—and he knew that the best way to speak to people is through the heart, jettisoning the argot of the specialist, the superiority of the self-righteous, and the sensationalism of the spiritual charlatan. He would be himself.

The decades-long quest to know himself was fraught with the unknown, the ugly, and the fearful, and he needed to make of this muck and mire a beautiful thing. Through painful transparency, he wrestled with his sexual identity, acknowledged his furiously buried failures of heart, experienced the leveling honesty of intensive therapy, and tried with near heroic fortitude to pave a road to holiness through the loneliness and abandonment that were his steady companions.

Nouwen was a cipher for the many who were drawn to him, because he represented their deepest but unarticulated yearnings, because he invested his suffering with meaning, because he could, through compassion, elevate his pain, alleviate the anguish of others, and open his own heart to that reciprocity that feeds our humanity.

But he also tasted failure regularly, saw himself as inadequate, and longed for a place he could call home, that could provide him with some surcease. He lived and functioned outside the boundaries that define most of us—hence the misfit—and like his mentors Kierkegaard and van Gogh, transmuted his personal pain into a universal truth. But unlike them, he never experienced the social and religious rejection they did, nor did he bring upon his head the severe displeasure of the ecclesiastical authorities of his time. In fact, in great measure he enjoyed their approval, if not occasional mystification. After all, Nouwen was an orthodox figure, distrustful of the cultural and ecclesial politics of the post–Second Vatican Council era, disinclined to throw himself into the controversies, theological and social, that flourished during his time, and fiercely determined to ensure that his reputation not be distilled or contracted by ideology or cause, no matter how worthy. He was a herald of the incontrovertible but rarely tasted truth of God's undifferentiating love.

That meant that Nouwen, the outsider, the misfit, knew that despite the darkness of depression, the night of God's absence, he would be the disciplined acrobat, the artist who relies on others but in the end remains the sole performer, *Le Jongleur de Dieu*, poised above the pit but incandescent with hope.

Afterword

Listening to Henri

I never met Henri. I remember reading his books and articles back in the1980s when I lived in western Canada. I recall thinking of him as a part of the Catholic furniture, someone who was just "there" whenever I took the time to notice. He was a familiar presence in the press. I can remember hearing him on the radio and seeing him in a few television clips. He was that Catholic priest and writer who instead of wearing a collar wore a long knitted scarf and who would come up with a new book every few years. Each new work would receive a lot of attention in both mainstream and Catholic newspapers, back in that pre-Internet era. Canadian Catholic journalism was in a very different state of health back then. I remember seeing posters, year after year, telling me that Henri would be giving the keynote address at this or that big conference. All I knew then of Henri Nouwen was the external, public image: a Dutch priest/psychologist, a charismatic and theatrical speaker who lived at L'Arche Daybreak, north of Toronto, and who raced all over the continent giving talks and retreats. He was (more or less) a Canadian celebrity who was also Catholic and who increasingly found audiences beyond the loose perimeters of the Canadian Catholic world. He was a rare thing at that time: an influential priest in the media and not in the crosshairs of controversy. And then there was this thing about him being a spiritual writer who had discovered some deep spiritual meaning at the circus.

Naturally, those limited perceptions changed the moment I began the serious work of preparing for and assembling a radio documentary about him more than a decade after his death. The documentary began with a shaky but memorable encounter. I had barely assembled some initial background material when, at a large Canadian university gathering, a young priest wearing his collar and clearly in some distress positioned himself in front of me at the hors d'oeuvres table. It had just been announced that Michael Higgins and I had been commissioned by the Canadian Broadcasting Corporation to prepare a three-part radio documentary on the life and legacy of Henri Nouwen. Red in the face and evidently struggling for control, the priest wagged a finger at me. "You media always get it wrong. I know what you are going to do. You are going to focus on the rumors and the gossip and distort the truth. You're all the same!"

I took a deep breath, smiled, and replied: "Well, I'll try my best not to disappoint you."

He walked away certain that he had been heard. And I walked away certain that I had been heard. And in a way we were both right. Listening can be like that. In that moment, each of us was listening in a kind of way, listening in order to hear only what we wanted to hear from the other, regardless of the words each of us may have been using. I think he probably heard opportunistic, sensationalist media hack with an agenda. I know I heard fear and repression. This experience of listening without hearing is nothing new in the Christian tradition, and neither is it limited to it. In the final verses of the Acts of the Apostles, we hear how Saint Paul struggled to be heard and understood clearly by those around him:

Some were convinced by what he had said, while others refused to believe.

So they disagreed with each other; and as they were leaving, Paul made one further statement: "The Holy Spirit was right in saying to your ancestors through the prophet Isaiah,

'Go to this people and say,
You will indeed listen, but never understand,
and you will indeed look, but never perceive.
For this people's heart has grown dull,
and their ears are hard of hearing,
and they have shut their eyes;
so that they might not look with their eyes,
and listen with their ears,
and understand with their heart and turn—
and I would heal them.'

Let it be known to you then that this salvation of God has been sent to the Gentiles; they will listen." (Acts 28: 24–28)

As we entered the final production phase of making the documentary, the phrase "understand with their heart, and turn" worked its way into my memory, like that wonderful German image of *der Ohrwurm,* or "ear worm," used to describe those pieces of music that can get stuck in your head.[1] To "understand with their heart and turn" captured for me something elemental about documentary production in general and also something fundamental about Henri. To struggle to understand with the heart and to work hard to find strength within in order to try and turn your life around seems to be a key element of his work, as a writer, as a priest, as a messenger, and as the message himself.

As I listened through the hiss and crackle of archival recordings of his talks and interviews (many of them recorded live and subject to distortion), I heard his remarkable energy and, at times, his exhaustion, the more I tried to understand the heart and mind of this complex and compelling individual.

This chapter is about what happened to me as, in order to understand more about him, I listened intently not only to Henri, but to the often passionate responses of those who knew him and his work intimately.

As a radio producer, when you record an interviewer and an interviewee, you spend hours with headphones clamped over your ears. You occasionally hear things that interviewers sometimes do not catch. You also hear the drone of a plane overhead as it slowly trails off in the distance. You hear the yappy dog barking three streets away. You hear the whine of a leaf-blower in the hands of an enthusiastic gardener in the yard across the fence. That's when you stop, even if it is at a critical time in the conversation. You remove your headset, sigh, and explain. Then you wait. You listen once more, check the sound meter, flip the still-warm headset over your ears once more, and you start again. A little while later, you hear the rumbling stomach of the interview subject who must have forgotten to have lunch or who maybe had too much lunch. Then you hear a forgotten cellphone as it vibrates in the pocket of whoever it is, this time, who has forgotten to turn it off. You hear the persistent hum of the air conditioning unit in the next room and the mosquito-like buzz of an aging fluorescent tube light above you. Now, there is a basic acoustic law in all audio production: every background sound eventually elbows its way to the front, and stays there. This is why during the production phase of the documentary, I would often move people from room to room and from space to space in order to find a suitable acoustic space where we might complete the interviews devoid of extraneous noises. It also explains why there are such things as radio studios. We used these whenever we could, but we also found that getting people to talk about Henri generally worked best in surroundings familiar to them—living rooms, dens, sitting at a kitchen table, and, of course, a chapel. Each of these spaces became a mobile studio and also a confessional of sorts. More on that in a moment.

Have you ever been inside a radio studio? They are often shabby, untidy places with fading carpet, threadbare furniture, forgotten coffee mugs, abandoned scripts, and lots of flickering colored lights on the recording equipment. They are also places of mystery where the outside world is not permitted to intrude. It may be snowing outside, with traffic snarled up for blocks, but we are deep in a conversation about the experience of having Henri Nouwen hear your confession. Nothing will interrupt this recall of a moment frozen in time and etched in memory. The impatient producer of a documentary on Iranian oil may be pacing outside, worried about phone lines, but we are winding up a conversation with Henri's editor who is telling us about the surprising challenges and career-changing insights that came to him as he worked with Henri the author and difficult friend. Then, our hour is up and the studio's red light goes off, and the interview is over. Only now is the outside world able to begin making its presence felt. What we found was that all of our conversations immediately following the recording sessions were, in fact, continuations of the interview. It was as if, having spent an hour with Henri in memory and reflection, they were not quite ready to let go of him just yet.

There is another surprising detail about the way broadcast media is produced, and it is this: for many people who are being interviewed, whether in the formality of a studio setting or on location somewhere, they focus so intently on the person asking the questions that they often forget about the presence of the other person who is working the equipment. This is a natural response, especially when that person is on the other side of the glass. Strangely, it works the same way when you record on location. I can report on my experience as the "tech" person for all the non-studio interviews. Whenever you play the role of the technician in an intimate interview, you can disappear in a room. It happens. Often. It's also true that, not being responsible for managing the flow of the conversation, you can listen differently. In addition to listening for those problematic extraneous sounds, when you monitor an interview through a headset and are controlling the recording levels, you also hear tiny openings that suddenly flicker in the middle of an answer. These take the form of a door that the person being interviewed has just opened up into a surprising personal depth and startling vulnerability, often in ways that catch everyone by surprise. Experienced interviewers, like Michael, will always find a way to open that door. That said, sometimes the focus of the interview requires the interviewer to put a "Do not disturb" sign on that particular door and to move on to avoid anecdotal diversions that will never be used.

I used the word *confessional* earlier to describe interviews, whether in the studio or on location. I learned from this project that to ask people to talk about Henri is to open up all sorts of personal and vulnerable doors. The wonderful, articulate people we interviewed would start off, clear, confident, calm, and very prepared. Then, all of sudden, we are no longer talking about a third party, Henri. We are talking about their own deep woundedness, their hopes, their uncertainties, their fears, their healing, their difficult journeys. It is no longer Henri's story that we are pursuing, but their own. We have begun to talk about their own deeply profound spiritual questions. All of a sudden, we are talking about fear, frailty, and loss, and the death of those we love dearly. No longer an abstract discussion with an expert on contemporary spirituality and mental health, this has become an intensely personal conversation about their own life. Talking about Henri taught me much about listening with more than my ears.

To call what we did in our interviews a technique or method does not quite capture the dynamic, but this is how we structured them: Michael and I would map out the expected content and scope for each interview, which we planned to record for an hour. Before we began recording, he would explain to our interviewees that I might come in at the end of the interview with a couple of questions of my own.

Interviews can be stressful, as they make people cautious about saying something stupid or just wrong. Interviews about Henri invariably relate to personal and spiritual experiences and the pursuit of meaning. After forty-five minutes of reflection, the dynamic of the interview has changed, as it is now a relaxed and candid conversation. Then, the previously invisible technician gets to ask his question at what seems to be the end of a formal interview. The effect of this second mini-interview was invariably revelatory, because these new questions, coming from someone who has been invisible up to that point, also come at a moment of highly focused concentration and intimate conversation. These final questions would take us back to some of those doors that were left open during the interview. As the "sound guy" I would also take notes during the interview and flag any potential doors left open along the way and frame my questions around them. For example, in his interview at L'Arche Daybreak, Nathan Ball used the language of swimming and lifesaving a couple of times as he recalled aspects of Henri's time there. Just saying, "So you were a lifesaver?" opened up new doors about images for living with this often difficult and charismatic individual. "I realized that this image of 'lifeguard' wasn't going to work. That wasn't something that I could do for fulfill...I don't know if I have a good metaphor." Talking in a dark, wood-paneled room at Yale's Thomas More Center, Kerry Robinson spoke about Henri as an expert. When I pointed out that this expertise was also coming from someone who was an ordained priest, she paused and said, "I don't even know that I've given it much thought, that he was a priest. It's more that he is an exemplary spiritual, mystical person that I find compelling." Ron Rolheiser was surprised when I reported back to him at the end of our interview in a Toronto studio that throughout the interview he kept talking about Henri in the present tense. Henri had been dead for well over a decade. "Then I'm glad, because with a Freudian slip I went in the right direction," he said with a deep smile. "You know, as Christians we remember the way Paul puts it so graphically in Thessalonians. He says as Christians we don't believe that those who are living are in any way advantaged or more alive than those who are dead."

No matter who asks the questions, after an hour of talking about Henri, our interview subjects had entered a place of deep and personal reflection. Henri seems to do that a lot, with people who knew him and with those who met him only through his books. We interviewed broadly in both groups. Not all of them are quoted in this book or in the documentary, but all of them are important because they helped us shape the work. Inevitably, large portions of interviews remain unused because they take us into a different theme, beyond the parameters of our series. Listening back to these interviews, I confess, I can hear moments where we both managed to miss a particular door as it opened, only for a fraction, right in front of our ears, as it were. Why? Because, no matter how intently an interviewer or producer might try, at that particular moment in the interview, you are actually listening for something else altogether. You are listening for what you would prefer to hear, listening for what you are hoping to hear, rather than what you are actually hearing right in front of you. The heart somehow stops understanding. And sometimes, no matter how long you talk and listen, every door remains firmly closed, locked so tight that you can only move on. To paraphrase Acts, this is when you may well be listening with your ears and understanding with your heart, but you still turn away.

Radio, like words on a page, can put instant pictures in your head and allow you to move Henri through time and across geography: from the Netherlands of his pre–Second World War childhood, his student life and call to the priesthood, to his time in the pomp and circumstance of Rome during the Second Vatican Council, to his arrival in the United States at a volatile time in the struggle for civil rights, and his clinical studies at the Menninger Clinic in Kansas at a turbulent moment in the history of the practice of psychological counseling. With a simple sound effect on radio, like a subheading on a page, we can jump to his short-lived excursions into the violence and oppression of Latin and South America in the troubled 1980s. The sound of a campus bell takes us to the lecture halls of Harvard and Yale. Another kind of bell takes us to the Abbey of Genesee, the place where Jean Vanier says, "You feel, though, he was never silent." The sound of a local commuter train takes us to the L'Arche community in northern France, where Vanier says Henri found "Something about discovery of meaning to community, to community life, seeing L'Arche also as a vision maybe for the future, for the Church." Birdsong and distant highway traffic take us to L'Arche Daybreak in Richmond Hill, Canada, where he lived and worked once again with people who are severely challenged, both mentally and physically. Our radio documentary, like this book, tells that biographical story through the interviews that we recorded and clips from excerpts from various radio and television archives. The series also includes a lot of different location sounds and music, which is slightly more difficult to deal with in print, but I am about to try.

We tell a mostly chronological story, one that begins in 1932 in the Netherlands on January 24, the feast day of St. Francis de Sales, who among other things is the patron saint of journalists and writers. We end with Henri Nouwen's death, alone in a hospital, on September 21, 1996, also in the Netherlands—where this prodigal son had stopped for a visit en route to Russia, where he was to make a documentary film on one of his favorite compatriot artists, Rembrandt. In between these chronological markers, we hear how people remember Henri.

Music plays an important role in this story, and not because of any importance it may have had in Henri's life. Gabrielle Earnshaw at the Henri Nouwen Archives showed me a single box of cassette tapes, many of which had been sent to Henri. I searched through this mix of commercial and homemade recordings of familiar classical pieces to find clues about Henri and music. Not finding much to work with, I decided to look for music that Henri might have heard wherever he lived. Here are just two examples of connections we make in this series with music and Henri.

I began with a work composed in 1927 by the Dutch composer Julius Röntgen (1855–1932), his Quintet for Piano and Strings in A Minor, Opus 100. I like to think of this as a piece of music that the young Henri, book in hand, could well have heard on the "wireless" in one of the various Nouwen households in the Netherlands. The music establishes time and place. It is also music that is unsettled, rest-less, headed somewhere into and beyond something that sounds like darkness. It's classical and traditional in form, yet it has a decidedly contemporary edge. Played on acoustic instruments, it is a natural, unprocessed sound. These descriptors also serve as words that capture something of Henri himself: unsettled, restless, headed somewhere into and beyond a certain darkness, someone who is traditional but with a decidedly contemporary edge. This is how a 45-second excerpt from the *Andante* movement became Henri's theme.[2]

The second example is surrounded in mystery. Little is known of the life of the English composer John Sheppard. His birth is guess-work, perhaps 1515. The few precise details are that from 1543 to 1548 he was the *Informator Choristarum*—the Director of Music—at Magdalen College in Oxford. Then he moved to London to become a Gentleman of the Chapel Royal under Queen Mary (Mary Queen of Scots, r. 1542–1567). His antiphon, *Media vita* ("In the midst of life we are in death") is one of the great vocal compositions in the history of liturgical music. Sheppard sets the Lenten prayer "*Sancte Deus, sancte fortis, sancte et misericors/Salvator, amarae morti ne tradas nos*" (Holy God, holy and strong, holy and merciful, do not hand us over to the bitter pains of death) to some remarkable, soaring music. Sheppard grabs your attention from his mysteriously quiet opening phrases, which he then fills with dissonant suspensions. Then, on four different occasions in this twenty-five-minute piece, he lets the vocal lines glide in an acoustic mix of danger and hope as he embellishes the phrase "Sancte Deus, sancte fortis, sancte et misericors/Salva-tor, amarae morti ne tradas nos." This is daring music with startling cumulative power. It requires vocalists to fly, confident that despite the risks of such an inherently complicated composition, they will arrive safely at the conclusion of the piece. In music performance there is rarely a safety net.

Media Vita is the theme we use for Henri's search for spiritual insight.[3] It introduces the section on Henri's exploration of the notion of the "flyer" and the "catcher" that was inspired by his encounter with the trapeze artist Rodleigh Stevens. In his *Circus Diary*, Henri wrote:

> I am convinced that I have been sent to the Rodleighs to discover something new about life and death, love and fear, peace and conflict, heaven and hell, something I can't get to know and write about in any other way. Often I think: "How could I have ever imagined, even a few years ago, that I would sit for a few weeks writing in a camper in the midst of a circus in Germany?" But here I am, and it feels like the only good place to be right now. What tomorrow will bring, I will find out tomorrow. I am happy that I don't have to know that today.[4]

Henri never completed the book he planned to write about the Flying Rodleighs. Shortly after learning of Henri's death, Rodleigh Stevens completed "What a Friend We Had in Henri," his interpretation of the encounter between trapeze artists and a charismatic priest.

> I am still mystified what it was about us which moved him enough to want to write about us. I can only presume that when he saw us working, he was able to put a visual aspect to his deep spiritual feelings. In other words, he could see something in us that he felt within himself and he had made a correlation between the two. We were merely the ingredients he needed to clarify those certain feelings, because I'm sure that it was more than just a boyhood fantasy to perform in a circus as a flier which attracted him to our troupe. When our friendship grew and we opened our homes and lives to him, he was able to live out certain religious aspects of his life through us. We could give him courage as he danced with us dangerously through the air. If we failed, we showed him that he could overcome the fear of failure and climb the ladder with us to try again.[5]

Life as a dangerous dance through the air with the possibility of failure, followed by another "go." This captures something elemental about Henri's life and work. In his talks and books, Henri describes people as "flyers" who need the confidence and trust that, when the time comes, they will be welcomed by the Almighty Catcher. Rodleigh's image "dangerously through the air" is also a way to capture Sheppard's *Media Vita* in its expression of that unknowable encounter between life and death: when the flyer is welcomed by the catcher. John Sheppard's music serves as a kind of theological leitmotif for Henri's insights into spirituality in each of the three episodes of the documentary. There's also (agreed, probably only) a slight chance that in the seminary in the Netherlands or while in Rome, Henri might have heard this sixteenth-century gem, even though it is not on any of the cassettes in his archive.

Unlike the challenges that a radio production has, it is much easier for a book to present visual art. We introduce each of the three main chapters with an iconic work from the visual artists who were Henri's lifelong companions and referred to often in his books and presentations: Rembrandt Harmenszoon van Rijn and Vincent van Gogh. Rembrandt's painting *The Return of the Prodigal Son* needs no further explanation here. Vincent van Gogh's *Shoes* (1886) captures the restless spirit of Henri's early life, while *The Fall of the Leaves* (*The Garden of Saint Paul's Hospital*, 1889), one of van Gogh's later works, shows someone, alone, surrounded by rich natural growth. It is not difficult to see Henri as that figure, only one foot on an established path.

Listening to Henri surfaced all manner of complementary and sometimes conflicting ideas about the paths of spirituality and mental health, about healing and woundedness, and about the difference between biography and hagiography. Given that the series our documentary was aired in is called *Ideas*, this brought some relief.

Ideas are not exactly finite things, though. Sometimes, in our interviews, the ideas being expressed were startlingly clear, sometimes confusing, and often still being formed as they were being reached for. Sometimes, like musical fragments, these ideas would be striking though fleeting, and sometimes they would linger long after the interview was over. Sometimes, an idea will just fade over time, slowly,

like an old photograph. Sometimes, an idea that has been let go early comes back in disguise. This, then, is not a conventional conclusion, but more of an expression of where Henri Nouwen's ideas have taken me after listening intently and immersing myself in his work and in the words of all those we spoke to about him.

Listening to Henri I have learned this:

- ❧ If I really want to listen, I need to invite silence so that I can hear what is being said, not only what I want or expect to hear.

- ❧ If I really want to listen, I have to slow things down and turn things off, metaphorically, not just literally.

- ❧ I've learned over and over again that somewhere in all of this is the conviction that to recognize a wound is to take a step in the direction of healing it.

- ❧ I've also learned that to listen is another form of prayer.

Not original, perhaps, but I am in good company, as this is also how Henri describes prayer—as a form of real listening. In 1981, he wrote that to listen is to move "from a life filled with noisy worries to a life in which there is some free inner space where we can listen to our God and follow…[God's] guidance."[6]

Working on this project has been both a professional and personal journey, a pilgrimage of sorts, and one that is perhaps as psychological as it is spiritual. No matter how we choose to label such a journey of investigation and exploration, it is one that is best guided by those who have bravely gone before us and who, through their art and their insights, are able to give creative guidance to those of us who are still stumbling on our way. This is what all true artists like Henri Nouwen can do for us. If we are willing to listen to them.

Notes

Chapter 1

1. Rex Murphy, *The Globe and Mail*, April 9, 2005.

2. James Roose-Evans, *The Tablet*, December 17–24, 2004.

3. Daniel O'Leary, *The Tablet*, April 18, 2009.

4. As quoted in Barbara Amiel's column, *Maclean's*, February 15, 2010.

5. As quoted in Clyde Haberman's column, *The New York Times*, February 5, 2010.

6. Donald Nicholl, "Holiness: A Call to Radical Loving," *Grail: An Ecumenical Journal* 4 (1989): 77–78.

7. Jean Vanier's Nouwen eulogy, September 25, 1996.

8. Michael O'Laughlin, *Henri Nouwen: His Life and Vision* (Maryknoll, NY: Orbis, 2005), 21.

9. John Dear, SJ, ed., *The Road to Peace: Writings on Peace and Justice* (Maryknoll, NY: Orbis, 1998), 26.

10. Jurjen Beumer, *Henri Nouwen: A Restless Seeking for God* (New York: Crossroad, 1997), 17.

11. Henri Nouwen, *Can You Drink the Cup?* (Notre Dame, IN: Ave Maria Press, 1996), 16.

12. John W. O'Mally, SJ, ed., *Vatican II: Did Anything Happen?* (New York: Continuum, 2007), 63–64.

13. Giuseppe Alberigo, *History of Vatican II, Volume 1: Announcing and Preparing Vatican Council II toward a New Era of Catholicism* (Maryknoll, NY: Orbis, 1995), 466–467.

14. Robert Adolfs, *The Grave of God: Has the Church a Future?* Translated by N. D. Smith (New York: Harper and Row, 1967), 11.

15. Anton Boisen, "The Form and Content of Schizophrenic Thinking," *Psychiatry: Journal of the Biology and Pathology of Interpersonal Relations* 5 (1942): 23.

16. Henri Nouwen, "Anton T. Boisen and Theology through Living Human Documents," *Pastoral Psychology* 19 (September 1968): 51.

17. Henri Nouwen, *Our Second Birth: Christian Reflections on Death and New Life* (New York: Crossroad, 2006), 24.

18. Henri Nouwen, *Intimacy* (New York: HarperOne, 1981), 23, 82, 97, 117, 150.

19. Henri Nouwen, *Encounters with Merton: Spiritual Reflections* (New York: Crossroad, 1981), 13.

20. Ibid., 75.

21. Michael Ford, *Wounded Prophet: A Portrait of Henri J. M. Nouwen* (New York: Doubleday, 1999), 119.

22. Raimundo Panikkar, *Blessed Simplicity: The Monk as Universal Archetype* (New York: Seabury Press, 1982), 11.

23. Henri Nouwen, *The Genesee Diary: Report from a Trappist Monastery* (New York: Doubleday, 1976), 182.

24. Henri Nouwen, *A Cry for Mercy: Prayers from the Genesee* (New York: Doubleday Image, 2002), 18, 36–37.

Chapter 2

1. Len Kofler, "First, Heal Yourself," *The Tablet*, July 4, 2009.

2. Henri Nouwen, *¡Gracias! A Latin American Journal* (Maryknoll, NY: Orbis, 2007), 188.

3. Ford, *Wounded Prophet*, 131.

4. John Garvey, "An Interview with Henri Nouwen," the rough draft of an article scheduled for publication in the University of Notre Dame alumni magazine and currently in the Henri J. M. Nouwen Archives, John M. Kelly Library, University of St. Michael's College, University of Toronto.

5. Robert A. Jonas, *Rebecca: A Father's Journey from Grief to Gratitude* (New York: Crossroad, 1996), xiii.

6. Cliff Edwards, *Van Gogh and God* (Chicago: Loyola University Press, 1989), x.

7. Ibid., ix, x.

8. O'Laughlin, *Henri Nouwen*, 83.

9. Parker J. Palmer, "The Violence of Our Knowledge: Toward a Spirituality of Higher Education," *Grail: An Ecumenical Journal* 2, no. 3 (September 1995): 112–113.

10. Henri J. M. Nouwen, *Lifesigns: Intimacy, Fecundity, and Ecstasy in Christian Perspective* (New York: Doubleday Image, 1986), 49–50.

11. Henri J. M. Nouwen, *The Road to Daybreak: A Spiritual Journey* (New York: Doubleday Image, 1988), 22.

12. Jean Vanier, *Lumen Vitae: International Review of Religious Education* 36, no. 4 (1981): 467, 470, 472, 474, 475.

13. Nouwen, *Lifesigns*, 51.

Chapter 3

1. Daniel O'Leary, *The Tablet*, February 4, 2012.

2. Gabrielle Earnshaw, *The Henri J. M. Nouwen Archives and Research Collection* (Toronto: John M. Kelly Library, 2011), 14.

3. Henri J. M. Nouwen, *Adam: God's Beloved* (Maryknoll, NY: Orbis, 1997), 15–16.

4. Henri J. M. Nouwen, *The Inner Voice of Love: A Journey through Anguish to Freedom* (New York: Doubleday Image, 1998), xv.

5. Ibid., xiv–xv.

6. Ibid., 109–110.

7. Ibid., 28–29.

8. Daniel O'Leary, *The Tablet*, December 17-24, 2011.

9. Earnshaw, *The Henri J. M. Nouwen Archives and Research Collection*, 16–17.

10. G. K. Chesterton, *St. Francis of Assisi* (London: Hodder and Stoughton, 1923), 79.

11. Henri J. M. Nouwen, *The Return of the Prodigal Son: A Story of Homecoming* (New York: Doubleday Image, 1994), 21.

12. Henri J. M. Nouwen, *Home Tonight: Further Reflections on the Parable of the Prodigal Son*, edited by Sue Mosteller, CSJ (New York: Doubleday, 2009), 130–131.

13. Nouwen, *Return of the Prodigal Son*, 123–124.

14. Henri J. M. Nouwen, *Beyond the Mirror: Reflections on Death and Life* (New York: Crossroad, 1992), 35.

15. Henri J. M. Nouwen, *Our Greatest Gift: A Meditation on Dying and Caring* (San Francisco: Harper San Francisco, 1994), 32.

16. Henri J. M. Nouwen, *Our Second Birth: Christian Reflections on Death and New Life* (New York: Crossroad, 2006), 189.

17. Private correspondence, January 30, 2012, between Larry Culliford and author.

18. Jean Vanier's eulogy for Henri Nouwen, September 25, 1996.

Afterword

1. Oliver Sacks, *Musicophilia: Tales of Music and the Brain* (New York: Knopf, 2007), 41–48.

2. Julius Röntgen, Quintet for Piano and String in A Minor, Opus 100, *Right Through the Bone*, ARC Ensemble, RCA Red Seal, 88697-15837-2, 2007, compact disc.

3. John Sheppard, *Media vita*, Stile Antico, Harmonia Mundi, HMU 807509, 2010, compact disc.

4. Henri Nouwen, "Circus Diary, Part II," *New Oxford Review* (July–August 1993): 8.

5. Rodleigh Stevens, "What a Friend We Had in Henri" (unpublished manuscript, n.d.).

6. Henri Nouwen, *Making All Things New* (New York: Harper and Row, 1981), 66–68.

The Interviews

This book and the radio documentary of the same name were built on interviews with the following people:

Nathan Ball, Director of the L'Arche Canada Foundation. Richmond Hill, Ontario. October 2008.

Fr. Robert L. Beloin, Catholic chaplain at Yale University. New Haven, Connecticut. June 2010.

Jurjen Beumer, Nouwen biographer, pastor, director of Stem in de Stad. Haarlem, Netherlands. October 2008.

Bill Clarke, SJ, chaplain to the International L'Arche movement. Guelph, Ontario. April 2009.

James Clarke, retired justice of the Supreme Court of Ontario, author. Guelph, Ontario. April 2009.

Dr. Larry Culliford, psychiatrist, co-founder of the United Kingdom's Royal College of Psychiatrists' Spirituality and Psychiatry Special Interest Group, and author. Sussex, England. October 2008.

Christopher De Bono, doctoral student, University of St. Michael's College in the University of Toronto. Toronto, Ontario. September 2010.

Gabrielle Earnshaw, Curator of Special Collections and Archivist of the Henri J. M. Nouwen Archives and Research Collection, University of St. Michael's College in the University of Toronto. Toronto, Ontario. April 2009.

Robert Ellsberg, publisher, Orbis Books. Maryknoll, New York. January 2009.

Dr. Margaret Farley, Senior Scholar in Theology and Medical Ethics and the Gilbert L. Stark Professor of Christian Ethics, Yale University, New Haven, Connecticut. Archived interview, December 2004.

John Garvey, regular columnist for *Commonweal,* long association with Nouwen, and priest of the Antiochan Orthodox Church. New York. February 2011.

Dr. Michael Hayes, former vice principal of St Mary's University College, Twickenham, London, now President of Mary Immaculate College. Limerick, Ireland. October 2008.

Robert A. Jonas, author, musician, and retreat leader. Founder of The Empty Bell. Northampton, Massachusetts. June 2010.

Sue Mosteller, CSJ, Henri Nouwen's Literary Executrix. Richmond Hill, Ontario. April 2009.

Dr. Peter Naus, retired professor of psychology, Chancellor Emeritus, St. Jerome's University. Waterloo, Ontario. April 2009.

Laurent Nouwen, Henri's brother. Rotterdam, Netherlands. October 2008.

Kerry Robinson, Executive Director of the National Leadership Roundtable on Church Management in the United States. New Haven, Connecticut. June 2010.

Ron Rolheiser, OMI, President of the Oblate School of Theology. San Antonio, Texas. August 2010.

Richard Sipe, former Benedictine, Certified Clinical Mental Health Counselor, author. La Jolla, California. December 2010.

Rodleigh Stevens, founder of the Flying Rodleighs Circus Troupe. Brisbane, Australia. April 2010.

Dr. Peter Tyler, Senior Lecturer in Pastoral Theology and Program Director for the MA in Pastoral Theology, St Mary's University College. Twickenham, London. October 2008.

Jean Vanier, founder of L'Arche. Trosly, France. May 2010.

Carolyn Whitney-Brown, author and former staff member of L'Arche Daybreak. Cowichan Bay, British Columbia. February 2010.

Henri Nouwen Resources

Books by Henri Nouwen

Henri Nouwen is a publisher's delight: a prolific author whose books continue to have remarkable shelf life, long after his death. The titles in this list indicate the extent of his past and present publishing success in the English language. Many of these titles are the result of co-publishing arrangements involving presses in the United States, the United Kingdom, Canada, and Australia, hence the multiple publisher listings for certain titles. Some of the original titles have been changed slightly over time, and certain works have been combined into new editions. Publishers continue to keep Nouwen on their front and backlists and new editions continue to appear. This selective list is organized alphabetically by title.

Adam: God's Beloved. Maryknoll, NY: Orbis Books, 1997; London: Darton, Longman and Todd, 1997; Blackburn, Vic. (Australia): HarperCollins Religious, 1997. Audio book: Cincinnati, OH: St. Anthony Messenger Press, 2007.

Aging and Ministry. Audio recording by Nouwen. Notre Dame, IN: Ave Maria Press, 1973.

Aging: The Fulfillment of Life. Garden City, NY: Doubleday, 1974, 1976. Audiocassette recorded by Nouwen: Notre Dame, IN: Ave Maria Press, 1973.

Arrivals and Departures: The Restless World of Henri Nouwen. Edited by Michael Ford. London: Darton, Longman and Todd, 2007.

Behold the Beauty of the Lord: Praying with Icons. Foreword by Robert Lentz. Notre Dame, IN: Ave Maria Press, 1987, 2007.

Beyond the Mirror: Reflections on Death and Life. London: Collins Fount, 1990; New York: Crossroad, 1990, 2001.

Bread for the Journey: Reflections for Every Day of the Year. London: Darton, Longman and Todd, 1996. Published as **Bread for the Journey: A Daybook of Wisdom and Faith,** San Francisco: Harper SanFrancisco, 1997.

Can You Drink the Cup? Foreword by Ron Hansen. Illustrations by Jane Pitz. Notre Dame, IN: Ave Maria Press, 1996, 2006.

Care and the Elderly. Richmond Hill, ON: Henri Nouwen Legacy Trust, 2008.

Circles of Love. Introduced and edited by John Garvey. London: Darton, Longman and Todd, 1988, 2004; Springfield, IL: Templegate, 1988.

Clowning in Rome: Reflections on Solitude, Celibacy, Prayer, and Contemplation. Garden City, NY: Image Books, 1979.

Compassion: A Reflection on the Christian Life. With Donald P. McNeill and Douglas A. Morrison. Drawings by Joel Filártiga. London: Darton, Longman and Todd, 1982, 2008; New York: Image Books/Doubleday, 2005.

Creative Ministry. Garden City, NY: Doubleday & Co, 1971, 1991.

Finding My Way Home: Pathways to Life and the Spirit. New York: Crossroad, 2001; London: Darton, Longman and Todd, 2001.

Finding Our Sacred Centre: A Journey to Inner Peace. Toronto: Novalis, 2011.

The Genesee Diary: Report from a Trappist Monastery. Garden City, NY: Image Books, 1981, 1976; New York/Toronto: Doubleday, 1989; London: Darton, Longman and Todd, 1995.

¡Gracias! A Latin American Journal. San Francisco/London: Harper & Row, 1983; Maryknoll, NY: Orbis Books, 1993.

Heart Speaks to Heart: Three Gospel Meditations on Jesus. Foreword by Christopher de Vinck. Notre Dame, IN: Ave Maria Press, 1989, 2007.

Here and Now: Living in the Spirit. New York: Crossroad, 1994; London: Darton, Longman and Todd, 1994. Audiobook: Cincinnati, OH: St. Anthony Messenger Press, 2000.

Home Tonight: Further Reflections on the Parable of the Prodigal Son. Edited by Sue Mosteller. New York: Doubleday, 2009; London: Darton, Longman and Todd, 2009. Audiobook: Escondido, CA: Hovel Audio, 2009.

In Memoriam. Notre Dame, IN: Ave Maria Press, 1980, 2005.

In the House of the Lord. London: Darton, Longman and Todd, 1986, 1997.

In the Name of Jesus: Reflections on Christian Leadership. New York: Crossroad, 1989, 1991; Darton, Longman and Todd, 1989.

The Inner Voice of Love: A Journey through Anguish to Freedom. New York: Doubleday/Image 1996, 1998; London: Darton, Longman and Todd, 1997. Audiobook: Cincinnati, OH: St. Anthony Messenger Press, 2001.

Intimacy: Essays in Pastoral Psychology. New York: Harper & Row, 1969, 1981.

A Letter of Consolation. San Francisco; London: Harper & Row, 1982, 2009; Dublin: Gill and Macmillan, c1983; Notre Dame, IN: Ave Maria Press, 2010.

Letters to Marc about Jesus. San Francisco: Harper & Row, 1988; Darton, Longman and Todd, 1988.

Life of the Beloved: Spiritual Living in a Secular World. New York: Crossroad, 1992; London: Hodder & Stoughton, 1993. Audiobook: Cincinnati, OH: St. Anthony Messenger Press, 2002.

Life of the Beloved. Combined edition with **Our Greatest Gift**. London: Hodder & Stoughton, 2002.

Living Reminder. Grand Rapids, MI: Zondervan, 2000.

Love in a Fearful Land: A Guatemalan Story. With photography by Peter K. Weiskel. Notre Dame, IN: Ave Maria Press, 1985; Maryknoll, NY: Orbis Books, 2006.

Making All Things New: An Invitation to the Spiritual Life. San Francisco: Harper & Row, 1981; Dublin: Gill and Macmillan/Washington, DC: Georgetown University Press, 1982; London: Fount, 2000.

My Sister, My Brother: Life Together in Christ. Ijamsville, MD: The Word Among Us Press, 2005.

Our Greatest Gift: A Meditation on Dying and Caring. London: Hodder & Stoughton, 1994; San Francisco: HarperSanFrancisco, 1994; New York: HarperOne, 2009. Audiobook: Cincinnati, OH: St. Anthony Messenger Press, 2000.

Our Second Birth: Christian Reflections on Death and New Life. New York: Crossroad, 2006

Out of Solitude: Three Meditations on the Christian Life. Notre Dame, IN: Ave Maria Press, 1974, 2004. Audiobook: Cincinnati, OH: St. Anthony Messenger Press, 2005.

The Path of Peace. New York: Crossroad, 1995; London: Darton, Longman and Todd, 1995.

The Path of Freedom. New York: Crossroad, 1995.

The Path of Power. New York: Crossroad, 1995; London: Darton, Longman and Todd, 1995.

The Path of Waiting. New York: Crossroad, 1995; London: Darton, Longman and Todd, 1995.

Peacework: Prayer, Resistance, Community. Foreword by John Dear, SJ. Maryknoll, NY: Orbis, 2005.

Pray to Live: Thomas Merton, A Contemplative Critic. Translated from the Dutch by David Schlaver. Notre Dame, IN: Ave Maria Press, 1972. Published as **Thomas Merton, Contemplative Critic**. San Francisco: Harper & Row, 1981; New York: Triumph Books, 1991; New York: Crossroad, 2004.

Reaching Out: The Three Movements of the Spiritual Life. Garden City, NY: Doubleday/Image Books, 1975, 1986; London: Collins, 1976, 1980. Audiobook: Cincinnati, OH: St. Anthony Messenger Press, 2001, 2005.

Reaching Out: A Special Edition of the Spiritual Classic Including Beyond the Mirror. With a personal appreciation by Gerard W. Hughes. London: Fount, 1998.

The Return of the Prodigal Son: A Meditation on Fathers, Brothers, and Sons. London: Darton, Longman and Todd, 1992; New York: Doubleday, 1992; New York: Continuum, 1995. Published as **The Return of the Prodigal Son: A Story of Homecoming**. New York: Image, 1993, 1994. Audiobook: Boulder, CO: Sounds True, 1998; Cincinnati, OH: St. Anthony Messenger Press, 2005.

The Road to Daybreak: A Spiritual Journey. New York/Toronto: Doubleday, 1988, 1990; London: Darton, Longman and Todd, 1989, 1997; New York: Continuum, 1997.

Sabbatical Journey: The Diary of his Final Year. New York: Crossroad, 1998. London: Darton, Longman and Todd, 1998.

The Selfless Way of Christ: Downward Mobility and the Spiritual Life. With illustrations by Vincent van Gogh. Maryknoll, NY: Orbis Books, 2007; London: Darton, Longman and Todd, 2007.

Show Me the Way. New York: Crossroad, 1992, 1995, 2002; London: Darton, Longman and Todd, 1993, 2005.

A Sorrow Shared: A Combined Edition of the Nouwen Classics: In Memoriam, and A Letter of Consolation. Foreword by Barbara Brown Taylor. Notre Dame, IN: Ave Maria Press, 2010.

Spiritual Direction: Wisdom for the Long Walk of Faith. With Michael J. Christensen and Rebecca J. Laird. San Francisco: HarperSanFrancisco, 2006.

Spiritual Formation: Following the Movements of the Spirit. With Michael J. Christensen and Rebecca J. Laird. New York: HarperOne, 2010.

A Spirituality of Caregiving. The Henri Nouwen Spirituality Series. Nashville: Upper Room Books, 2011.

A Spirituality of Fundraising. Toronto: The Henri Nouwen Society, 2004; Nashville: Upper Room Books, 2010.

A Spirituality of Living. Nashville: Upper Room Books, 2012.

Spirituality of Marriage and the Family. Audio recording by Nouwen. Notre Dame, IN: Ave Maria Press, 1976.

Walk with Jesus: Stations of the Cross. With illustrations by Helen David. Maryknoll, NY: Orbis Books, 1990.

The Way of the Heart: Desert Spirituality and Contemporary Ministry. London: Darton, Longman and Todd, 1981, 1999; San Francisco: HarperSanFrancisco, 1991. Published as **The Way of the Heart: The Spirituality of the Desert Fathers and Mothers**. New York: Harper-One, 1981, 2009.

With Burning Hearts: A Meditation on the Eucharistic Life. Maryknoll, NY: Orbis Books, 1994, 2003; London: Geoffrey Chapman, 1994. Audiobook: Cincinnati, OH: St. Anthony Messenger Press, 2005.

With Open Hands. Notre Dame, IN: Ave Maria Press, 1972, 1995, 2006.

The Wounded Healer: Ministry in Contemporary Society. Garden City, NY: Doubleday, 1972, 1979; London: Darton, Longman and Todd, 1979, 1994.

Books with a Foreword, Preface, or Introduction by Henri Nouwen

Brother Lawrence of the Resurrection. **The Practice of the Presence of God**. Translated with an introduction by John J. Delaney. Foreword by Henri Nouwen. New York/London: Image Books, 1977.

Buser, Christella. **Flowers from the Ark: True Stories from the Homes of L'Arche**. Foreword by Jean Vanier. Afterword by Henri Nouwen. New York: Paulist Press, 1996.

Dufresne, Edward R. **Partnership: Marriage and the Committed Life**. Photographs by John Foraste. Foreword by Henri Nouwen. New York: Paulist Press, 1975.

Francis de Sales and Jane de Chantal, **Letters of Spiritual Direction**. Selected and introduced by Wendy M. Wright and Joseph F Power. Translated by Péronne Marie Thibert. Preface by Henri Nouwen. New York: Paulist Press, 1988.

Jonas, Robert A. Rebecca: **A Father's Journey from Grief to Gratitude**. New York: Crossroad, 1996.

Lucey, Rose Marciano. **Roots and Wings: Dreamers and Doers of the Christian Family Movement**. Foreword by Henri Nouwen. San Jose, CA: Resource Publications, Inc., 1987.

Matthew the Poor. **The Communion of Love**. Introduction by Henri Nouwen. Crestwood, NY: St. Vladimir's Seminary Press, 1984.

Palmer, Parker J. **The Promise of Paradox: A Celebration of Contradictions in the Christian Life**. Foreword by Henri Nouwen. Notre Dame, IN: Ave Maria Press, 1980.

Romero, Oscar. **The Church Is All of You**. Compiled and translated by James R. Brockman. Foreword by Henri Nouwen. London: Fount Paperbacks, 1984, 1985.

Thompson, Marjorie J. **Soul Feast: An Invitation to the Christian Spiritual Life**. Foreword by Henri Nouwen. Louisville, KY: Westminster John Knox Press, 1995.

Turner, Gordon Bruce. **Outside Looking In**. Foreword by Henri Nouwen. Toronto: United Church Publishing House, 1987.

Vanier, Jean. **Man and Woman He Made Them**. Foreword by Henri Nouwen. London: Darton, Longman and Todd, 1985. Republished as **Man and Woman God Made Them**. Mahwah, NJ: Paulist, 2008; London: Darton, Longman and Todd, 2008; Toronto: Novalis, 2008.

Vanderwall, Francis W. **Spiritual Direction: An Invitation to Abundant Life**. Foreword by Henri Nouwen. New York: Paulist Press, 1981.

Excerpts and Anthologies

Arrivals and Departures: The Restless World of Henri Nouwen. Edited by Michael Ford. London: Darton, Longman and Todd, 2007.

Beauty of the Beloved: A Henri Nouwen Anthology. Edited by Robert A. Jonas. London: Darton, Longman and Todd, 1999.

Be with Me, Lord: Prayers and Reflections for the Advent Season. Edited by James E. Adams. St. Louis, MO: Creative Communications, 1998.

Circles of Love: Daily Readings with Henri Nouwen. Edited by John Garvey. London: Darton, Longman and Todd, 1988, 2004; Springfield, IL: Templegate, 1988.

The Dance of Life: Spiritual Direction with Henri Nouwen. Edited by Michael Ford. London: Darton, Longman and Todd, 2005. Published as The Dance of Life: Weaving Sorrows and Blessings into One Joyful Step. Notre Dame, IN: Ave Maria Press, 2005.

The Essential Henri Nouwen. Edited by Robert A. Jonas. Boston/London: Shambhala, 2009.

Eternal Seasons: A Spiritual Journey through the Church's Year with Henri Nouwen. Edited by Michael Fore. Notre Dame, IN: Ave Maria Press, 2007.

The Heart of Henri Nouwen: His Words of Blessing. Edited by Rebecca Laird and Michael J. Christensen. New York: Crossroad, 2003. London: Darton, Longman and Todd, 2004.

Henri Nouwen: A Book of Hours. Compiled by Robert Waldron. London: Darton, Longman and Todd, 2009; New York: Seabury Books, 2009; Toronto: Novalis, 2009.

Henri Nouwen Illuminated. Edited and illustrated by Len Sroka. Skokie, IL: ACTA Publications, 2005.

Henri Nouwen: In My Own Words. Compiled and edited by Robert Durback. Liguori, MO: Liguori, 2001; London: Darton, Longman and Todd, 2002.

Henri Nouwen: Writings. Selected with an introduction by Robert A. Jonas. Maryknoll, NY: Orbis Books, 1998.

An Hour with Henri Nouwen. Edited by Judith A. Bauer. Liguori, MO: Liguori, 2005.

Jesus: A Gospel. Edited by Michael O'Laughlin. Maryknoll, NY: Orbis, 2001.

In Joyful Hope: Meditations for Advent. Edited by James E. Adams. St. Louis, MO: Creative Communications, 1997.

Living the Beatitudes: Daily Reflections for Lent. Compiled by the L'Arche Daybreak Community. Foreword by Henri Nouwen. Cincinnati, OH: St. Anthony Messenger Press, 1995.

The Lord Is Near: Advent Meditations from the Works of Henri Nouwen. Edited by Mark Neilsen. Fenton, MO: Creative Communications, 2001.

The Only Necessary Thing: Living a Prayerful Life. Edited by Wendy Wilson Greet. New York: Crossroad, 1999; London: Darton, Longman and Todd, 1999, 2000.

Renewed for Life: Daily Lenten Meditations from the Works of Henri Nouwen. Edited by Mark Neilsen. Fenton, MO: Creative Communications, 2003.

A Retreat with Henri Nouwen: Reclaiming Our Humanity. Edited by Robert Durback. Cincinnati, OH: St. Anthony Messenger Press, 2003; London: Darton, Longman and Todd, 2003.

The Road to Peace: Writings on Peace and Justice. Edited by John Dear. Maryknoll, NY: Orbis, 1998, 2005.

Seeds of Hope: A Henri Nouwen Reader. Edited by Robert Durback. Foreword by Mary Craig. Toronto/New York: Bantam Books, 1989; London: Darton, Longman and Todd, 1989, 1998.

Turn My Mourning into Dancing: Moving through Hard Times with Hope. Compiled and edited by Timothy Jones. Nashville: W Pub. Group, 2001.

Words of Hope and Healing: 99 Sayings. Edited by Jeff Imbach. Hyde Park, NY: New City Press, 2005.

Henri Nouwen on Audio and Video

The most comprehensive collection of audio and video recordings of Henri Nouwen remains in archival collections, because many of them were made in the era of audio- and videocassette recording and duplication and the growth of audiobook production. Relatively few of these recordings have made the transition to digital or commercially available formats.

The most complete listing of archival recordings by far, both video and audio, is found in the Henri J. M. Nouwen Archives at the John M. Kelly Library, University of St. Michael's College in the University of Toronto. Rather than reprint their extensive lists here, we encourage you to consult the collection online.

http://stmikes.utoronto.ca/kelly/nouwen/doc/1.10.Videorecordings.pdf (accurate as of June 2012)

http://stmikes.utoronto.ca/kelly/nouwen/

The Henri Nouwen Society has made a collection of short videos available on its website:

http://www.henrinouwen.org/Video_Audio/Videos/Videos.aspx (accurate as of June 2012).

The selection includes an excerpt from a 2009 Salt and Light Television series, *Witness*, with Sue Mosteller, and another presentation on "The Spirituality of Fundraising" for the Diocese of Camden, New Jersey, the same year. There's also a clip from 1991 with Henri Nouwen commenting on being awarded an Honorary Doctor of Humane Letters from Earlham College, Richmond, Indiana.

In 1994, Henri received The Comiss Award, presented periodically to a person who has made an outstanding contribution to the field of Pastoral Care, Counseling and Education, recorded in Milwaukee. Finally, there an excerpt from a workshop with Henri on the parable of the Prodigal Son, which became the basis of *Home Tonight*, edited by Sue Mosteller.

Here is a selection of recordings that are available commercially; some of them may be difficult to track down.

Video

Angels over the Net. Produced by Media Producties Netherlands, in 1995 and released as a 30-minute VHS format video for L'Arche Daybreak to sell in Canada.

Being the Beloved. Produced by Crystal Cathedral Ministries in 1992 for Robert Schuller's Crystal Cathedral Video Series (#1177), this is a video recording of a live homiletic presentation by Henri Nouwen.

From the House of Fear to the House of Love: A Spirituality of Peacemaking. Produced by the Missionary Society of St. Paul in 2002, this is a video recording of Henri Nouwen speaking about "intimacy that leads to solidarity" and "fecundity that calls us to receive the gifts of the poor and the struggles of people for our own conversion." Center for Social Concerns, University of Notre Dame, IN.

Open Hearts, Open Minds, Open Doors. A 1997 video production published in partnership with the Catholic Archdiocese of Chicago to celebrate the work of Joseph Cardinal Bernardin and Father Henri Nouwen and with a focus on the inclusion of persons with physical, mental, and other challenges in worship and church life. Produced by Pathways Awareness Foundation, Chicago.

Journey of the Heart: The Life of Henri Nouwen. A 56-minute video documentary narrated by Susan Sarandon, aired on PBS in 2007. Directed by Karen Pascal, and produced by Windbourne Productions of Markham, Ontario, Canada.

An Evening with Rev. Henri Nouwen. A 62-minute video recording of Henri Nouwen's presentation in 1994 on the **Return of the Prodigal Son** and related themes. Produced for L'Arche Mobile, AL.

Audio

Although there are some relatively early examples of "talking book" audiocassettes now long out-of-print in the Nouwen Archives, unlike the situation with video, there is a growing catalogue of audio CDs featuring the voice of Henri Nouwen. Most are location recordings of him giving talks and presentations to various groups, with the exception of the first item in this list:

Beloved: Henri Nouwen in Conversation with Philip Roderick. This is a book that contains the transcript of a conversation between Nouwen and Roderick, which is also included in audio on a CD. Originally produced by Canterbury Press in the United Kingdom in 2007, it was also co-published by Novalis in Canada and by William B. Eerdmans in the United States.

Who Will Mourn My Dance?
Desert Spirituality and Contemporary Ministry
Who Are We?—Exploring Our Christian Identity
The Lonely Search for God
A Spirituality of Waiting

A series of audio CDs featuring talks and presentations by Henri Nouwen, released in 2006 by Ave Maria Press, Notre Dame, IN.

The Henri Nouwen Society also posts short audio clips on its website: http://www.henrinouwen.org/. Here, amongst others, you can hear Henri Nouwen reflecting on the death of Dr. Martin Luther King that was later included in *The Road to Peace*, published by Orbis in 1998.

Books about Henri Nouwen

Bengtson, Jonathan and Gabrielle Earnshaw, eds. **Turning the Wheel: Henri Nouwen and Our Search for God.** New York: Orbis/Ottawa: Novalis, 2007.

Beumer, Jurjen. **Henri Nouwen: A Restless Seeking for God.** Translated from the Dutch by David E. Schlaver and Nancy Forest-Flier. New York: Crossroad, 1997.

Earnshaw, Gabrielle. **The Henri J. M. Nouwen Archives and Research Collection.** Toronto: John M. Kelly Library, University of St. Michael's College, 2011.

Ford, Michael. **Wounded Prophet: A Portrait of Henri Nouwen.** London: Darton, Longman and Todd, 1999.

Glaser, Chris. **Henri's Mantle: 100 Meditations on Nouwen's Legacy.** Cleveland, OH: Pilgrim Press, 2002.

Hernandez, Wil. **Henri Nouwen: A Spirituality of Imperfection.** New York: Paulist Press, 2006.

———. **Henri Nouwen and Soul Care: A Ministry of Integration**. New York: Paulist Press, 2008.

———. **Henri Nouwen and Spiritual Polarities: A Life of Tension**. New York: Paulist Press, 2012.

LaNoue, Deirdre. **The Spiritual Legacy of Henri Nouwen**. New York/London: Continuum, 2000.

O'Laughlin, Michael. **God's Beloved: A Spiritual Biography of Henri Nouwen**. Maryknoll, NY: Orbis, 2004.

———. **Henri Nouwen: His Life and Vision**. London: Darton, Longman and Todd, 2005.

O'Rourke, Michelle. **Befriending Death: Henri Nouwen and a Spirituality of Dying**. Toronto: Novalis/Maryknoll, NY: Orbis, 2009.

Porter, Beth, ed. **Befriending Life: Encounters with Henri Nouwen**. With Susan M. S. Brown and Philip Coulter. New York: Doubleday, 2001.

Ringma, Charles. **Dare to Journey with Henri Nouwen**. Oxford: Lion, 1992. Colorado Springs, CO: Pinon Press, 2000.

———. **The Seeking Heart: A Journey with Henri Nouwen**. Brewster, MA: Paraclete Press, 2006.

Roderick, Philip. **Beloved: Henri Nouwen in Conversation**. Norwich, UK: Canterbury Press, 2007 (book with audio CD).

Ruddle, William. **Henri Nouwen: Wounded Healer**. Cambridge: Grove Books, 2005.

Twomey, Gerald S. and Claude Pomerleau, eds. **Remembering Henri: The Life and Legacy of Henri Nouwen**. New York: Orbis/Toronto: Novalis, 2006.

de Vinck, Christopher, ed. **Nouwen Then: Personal Reflections on Henri**. Grand Rapids, MI: Zondervan, 1999.

Waldron, Robert. **15 Days of Prayer with Henri Nouwen**. Hyde Park, NY: New City Press, 2009.

———. **Walking with Henri Nouwen: A Reflective Journey**. New York: Paulist Press, 2003.

Nouwen is also presented in these works:

Ellsberg, Robert, ed. **Modern Spiritual Masters: Writings on Contemplation and Compassion**. Maryknoll, NY: Orbis, 2008.

———. **The Saints' Guide to Happiness: Everyday Wisdom from the Lives of the Saints**. New York: North Point Press/ Farrar, Straus and Giroux, 2003.

Layout by Audrey Wells
Cover design: Angel Guerra (Canadian edition); Lynn Else (US edition)

ISBN 978-0-8091-4785-4

Higgins, Michael W.
Genius born of anguish : the life and legacy of Henri Nouwen / Michael W. Higgins and Kevin Burns.
    p. cm.
Includes bibliographical references.
ISBN 978-0-8091-4785-4 (alk. paper)
1. Nouwen, Henri J. M. I. Burns, Kevin, 1952 - II. Title.
BX4705.N87H54 2012
282.092—dc23
[B]

2012018350

Published by Paulist Press
997 Macarthur Boulevard
Mahwah, New Jersey 07430
www.paulistpress.com

Published in Canada by Novalis

Publishing Office
10 Lower Spadina Avenue, Suite 400
Toronto, Ontario, Canada
M5V 2Z2

Head Office
4475 Frontenac Street
Montréal, Québec, Canada
H2H 2S2

www.novalis.ca

Library and Archives Canada Cataloguing in Publication

Higgins, Michael W.
    Genius born of anguish : the life and legacy of Henri
Nouwen / Michael W. Higgins and Kevin Burns.

Co-published by: Paulist Press.
Includes bibliographical references.
ISBN 978-2-89646-472-2

    1. Nouwen, Henri J. M. 2. Spiritual life--Catholic Church.
3. Catholic Church--Canada--Clergy--Biography. 4. Catholic
Church--Netherlands--Clergy--Biography. I. Burns, Kevin, 1952-
II. Title.

BX4705.N87H53 2012   282.092   C2012-903405-3

Printed in Canada.

We acknowledge the financial support of the Government of Canada through the Canada Book Fund for business development activities.

Genius Born
of Anguish

The Life & Legacy
of Henri Nouwen

Michael W. Higgins
& Kevin Burns

Paulist Press
New York / Mahwah, NJ

NOVALIS